GRELEASING THE GUARDS

CHRISTOPHER J. GOODEN

CREATION
H O U S E
A STRANG COMPANY

RELEASING THE GUARDS by Christopher J. Gooden
Published by Creation House
A Strang Company
600 Rinehart Road
Lake Mary, Florida 32746
www.strangbookgroup.com

Unless otherwise noted, Scripture quotations are from the Holy Bible, New International Version. Copyright © 1973, 1978, 1984, International Bible Society. Used by permission.

Scripture quotations marked KJV are from the King James Version of the Bible.

Scripture quotations marked NKJV are from the New King James Version of the Bible. Copyright © 1979, 1980, 1982 by Thomas Nelson, Inc., publishers. Used by permission.

Design Director: Bill Johnson
Cover design by Karen Gonsalves

Library of Congress Control Number: 2009929608
International Standard Book Number: 978-1-59979-862-2

First Edition

09 10 11 12 13 — 9 8 7 6 5 4 3 2 1
Printed in the United States of America

CONTENTS

DEDICATION

BEFORE BEGINNING MY dedications I want to offer to my family and friends a sincere apology for the pain you unnecessarily endured because of me. I realize how completely wrong and utterly selfish my actions have been over the years. It is my undeserved desire that you some way find it in your hearts to forgive me for my insensitive and at times cruel behavior. I deeply regret allowing my circumstances to dictate my emotions such that I took my pain and anger out on you. Again, please search your hearts and somehow find a path to forgive me.

To my sister Pat: you are so many things to me. Most importantly, you are a hero. The consistent manner in which you live your life honoring God is a premier example. I love you and thank God for you. I am entirely honored to be your little brother.

To Barbara: my wonderful friend, you said this was to be my journey. You are one of my angels. I would never have taken this path without your support, guidance, and certainly without the unconditional love you modeled and offered, especially when I was so undeserving. You have my eternal gratitude and you must know, I love you dearly.

To Jim and KC: I will remain eternally grateful for the steadfast support you have given me. It is my prayer that God will allow me to bless your family as you have so unselfishly blessed my life. I wish to thank you Jim for your patience. It is obvious God touched your heart throughout this process. I admire the way you opened your heart to this project especially since you had no reason to do so. To God be the glory.

To Kenny: my brother and my rock, there were so many times I felt defeated and alone. You unstintingly have been there for me and picked me up during those times when I felt broken and wanted to give in. Your encouragement and undying support are major contributors to my growth. Thank you for showing me a man's love.

To Reggie: my brother and friend. I remember telling you about my abuse. The way you embraced me with notable thoughtfulness left an indelible impression. The consistent concern you have shown for my plight will never go unnoticed and will always—always—be appreciated.

To Kim: I wish to thank you for opening my heart and allowing me to experience a joy I never achieved before you. The love I realized for you will forever remain in my heart. I will always cherish the time we had together. I pray God's endless blessing be upon you always.

To Mike: my friend and brother in Christ. Thank you for your insights. I have always admired your ability to show incredible concern and empathy for your fellow man. Thanks for sharing God's love and for being an unbelievable example of how to sacrifice your personal desires to do God's will.

To Petals: the very moment we met, you impacted my life. You renewed my spirit and opened my heart. I have an abundance of gratitude for the manner in which you showed your love and kindness. You will forever hold a very special place in my heart. I love you.

To Nina: what a wonderful little sister you have become. You have shown me an enriching love. Your presence in my life brings me great joy. It is my sincere hope that your heart experiences all of the happiness you give to others. I love you, sis'.

To Phyllis: your unassuming spirit is exceptionally inspiring. To that end, I submit to you, it is very easy to believe in God, when I know an angel.

To my Lord and Savior Jesus Christ: I bless You, Lord, and with great certainty I love You with my entire heart. Thank You for my deliverance, healing, and salvation.

INTRODUCTION

THIS IS MY testimony, if you will, of how God delivered me from the throws of a gripping self-hatred and damning violence into a life of satisfying peace and longed for self-control. I was sexually abused as a child. While this is my story, my circumstances are not unique. I am only one of what may be millions of victims of sexual abuse. The many issues to be discussed in this story are also shared by many of these same victims.

My name is Christopher Jerome Gooden and I am a recovering victim of sexual abuse.

More than society wants to believe, sexual abuse has impacted the lives of many innocent people, inflicting long-term, devastating consequences on its victims. Sexual abuse occurs when "an adult...touches or fondles in a sexual way, and/or had you touch their body in a sexual way, and/or attempted or actually had intercourse."[1] Sexual abuse may also include having children pose or undress in a sexual fashion on film or in person and exposing children to adult sexual activity.

Statistics reveal that, "one out of four females...and one out of six males will be sexually abused."[2] It is also believed that these individuals will be victimized before turning eighteen. As a Clinical Social Worker and a victim of sexual abuse, these statistics are not so surprising. But to demonstrate the significance of this problem, I will use some hypothetical numbers to suggest its overwhelming prevalence.

Let us assume an average high school classroom will have anywhere from twenty-eight to thirty students. Let us also assume, for the sake of argument, the classes are split 53 percent girls and 47 percent boys (there are generally more girls than boys in classrooms). In an average classroom of thirty students, that would be approximately sixteen girls and fourteen boys. If these statistics are correct, then four out of the sixteen girls and roughly three out of the fourteen boys in each classroom will experience some form of sexual abuse before turning eighteen.

To extend this discussion even further, let us assume the student population in a high school may average approximately one thousand students. Assuming the previously mentioned percentages with regard to girls and boys, this school would consist of 530 girls and 470 boys. This would mean in a high school with a population of one thousand students, 133 of the girls and 78 of the boys will experience some form of sexual abuse by the age of eighteen. This would also mean close to 21 percent of this school's entire population will experience some form of sexual abuse.

These are horrendous statistics. It is my contention that as staggering as these projections are, they are probably erring on the lower side because so many victims of sexual abuse do not report their experiences.

In January 1998, at almost forty years old, I was invited to speak before my church congregation as a part of our Black History Month celebration. As befitting my normal protocol, I spent several days deciding on a topic before preparing for my speech. As I considered a variety of topics, it became apparent that a growing desire was leading me to discuss the abusive nature of slavery and the emotional scars left on African Americans.

As I reflected on the lingering issues related to slavery, I began to realize there were very real and definite parallels to my life as a child, and more specifically clear parallels to my life as an abused child. Without going into great detail at this time, several similar issues that began to surface were a developed self-hatred, a sickened sense of loyalty to abusers, self-esteem as it related to pride and/or a lack of pride, self-worth issues, anger, and aggression just to name a few.

During the presentation I discussed the enduring issues related to slavery and drew parallels to my own abuse. To that end the presentation went very well. I was left that evening, however, wrestling with my own issues. I was truly faced with a decision to continue living a guarded and calculated life, or choosing to finally take control of my life, my emotions, and my future. I had been involved in counseling several times and to some degree I felt like I had been healed from my abuse. But the more time I spent that evening reflecting on my life, the more I realized it was time for me to honestly examine my life and myself. It was time to make the hard decisions as they related to me as well as to my family and those individuals responsible for my abuse.

At the age of nine early in my third grade year, what was once a safe and innocent world quickly became dreadfully dark and confusing. I was sexually molested by two male relatives and this incredibly horrid crime continued for more than a year. During that time, due to the extreme and disgusting physical nature of sexual abuse, I became immeasurably, emotionally, and physically drained. At best I would describe my condition during that period as severely fragile. With a profound fear from the threats by my perpetrators and an all-consuming shame preventing me from telling family members, I was left to survive in what became a cold and lonely world...on my own.

After spending the majority of the evening reflecting on my life, I decided I would make the hard decisions. I knew in my heart I wanted complete healing from my sexual abuse. I desired peace of mind and I needed the perpetrators to know I remembered what they did to me, but not for the sake of revenge. You see I had come to realize my peace was going to be contingent upon my forgiveness. Even though I knew this, it was because I continuously struggled with this fact that it remained one of the major contributors to my not dealing with my abuse. I did not want to forgive the individuals who violated me and I wanted them as well as other family members to pay for what I had to endure as a nine-year-old defenseless child.

Despite these facts, the purpose of this text is not to identify or vilify the persons who abused me. They have to deal with their own truths. It is my desire through this story to discuss truths about sexual abuse, the reality that many children are sexually abused, to help prevent sexual abuse, and most importantly, to show healing from sexual abuse is achievable.

After hours of deliberation, something I was faced with throughout my counseling had begun to eat away at me. This was the fact that I would eventually have to confront the persons who abused me. I eventually came to terms with making my first hard decision and it was to finally move forward with the confrontation. I chose to do this in a letter. I spent that evening writing two separate letters to those individuals. The letters were very specific, replete with details as they related to the abuse and as they related the monumental impact their abuse has had on my life.

I will always remember the taxing weight of emotions I experienced the next morning as I prepared to drop the letters into the mailbox. I began to sweat and shake. I remember an indescribable fear as I wondered how I would handle being rejected, or how I would deal with everyone knowing the shameful secret with which I lived for almost thirty-one years. I wondered if I was being selfish or if my actions were going to ruin my family.

I stood at that mailbox for more than an hour before depositing those letters. After dropping them into the mailbox, my fear still drove me to attempt to retrieve them. Unable to retrieve the letters, I stood by the mailbox and prayed to God to not only begin my complete healing, but to somehow also bring healing to my family and to those individuals who abused me.

One of the most significant fundamentals of my faith is that I believe life is about choices. This belief has evolved from my appreciation of the Serenity Prayer, which reads, "God give me the serenity to accept things which cannot be changed; Give me courage to change things which must be changed; And the wisdom to distinguish one from the other."[3]

We have all at some point in our lives had difficult or tragic experiences wherein we were left feeling life simply is not fair. Having been a victim of sexual abuse, I clearly lived a great part of my life trying to understand why I had to endure such a fate. I always felt like my experiences were the worst of the worst, giving way sometimes only to things like terminal diseases and physical disabilities. But as I have grown older, I have had the opportunity to see that everyone has life-changing experiences. Some may be different from mine, and as I often thought when I was younger, some people's experiences were not as bad as mine, either. I now realize the latter part of that statement is selfish and untrue.

Try as we may, we cannot completely control our fate, our destiny, or our circumstances. I am not saying we are helpless here, as I do recognize we can impact our life and in many ways affect a great deal of our circumstances. However, there will always be things to happen in our lives—whether they make sense or not, whether or not they seem fair—that will always challenge our resolve. It is this part of our lives that I am speaking about, the times when we are left defenseless, feeling alone, helpless, and defeated by our circumstances. This is when our true self has to step up, when we have to fight our best fight to overcome adversity and what may appear to be insurmountable odds.

Another of my favorite quotes is "That which does not destroy us makes us stronger."[4] During the times when our resolve is trying to fold and hope is waning as we are in the throws of our hardships, I believe we come face to face with only two choices. We are either going to fight against, or give in to, our circumstances. I am not saying that if we choose to fight we will always win. But I am saying that, by fighting, we at least give ourselves a chance to win. Giving up cannot be an option.

For almost thirty-one years I struggled to maintain a consistent fight to overcome my sexual abuse. My emotional resolve was often weak and I lacked courage and self-confidence. I found it easier to give up and throw myself frequent pity parties. It is so easy to get people to feel sorry for you, especially when you can get them to see your pain. Not until I decided with my entire being that I could heal, that I deserved to heal, and I was going to allow myself to heal, was I able to begin my current path to deliverance and healing. It was *a choice* I had to make in order to survive in this world because the emotions from my child abuse were like a cancerous growth, slowly eating away at my mind, body, and soul. It was *a choice* I made to allow God to be my Guide on a journey that ultimately led to healing.

I do not believe my resolve is any stronger than the next person's. The Word of God reads in 1 Corinthians 10:13, "God is faithful; he will not let you be tempted beyond what you can bear." I understand now that we all have different resolves that enable us to handle different circumstances in different ways. What may be easy for me to handle may be hard for someone else. Conversely, what may be easy for one person to handle may be extremely difficult for me.

We owe it to ourselves to at least try, when it appears there is no way we can defeat our circumstances. We must force ourselves to make the tough decisions and choose to do the things, no matter how difficult, that will make us overcomers and enable us to live thriving lives. Philippians 4:13 reads, "I can do everything through him who gives me strength." It is from this ultimate reflection that the motivation for this text is derived from the following:

...there go I, but for the grace of God.

This poem is dedicated to all abused children:

FAMILIAR STRANGER

At thirteen you called me Daddy's girl
and always held me tight.
I trusted you not knowing
your plans for me one night.

A secret lives in my bedroom
and if only those walls could talk,
then just maybe they would have warned me
something strange was in your walk.

Many times you looked in on me
always making me feel safe.
This time your reason was different
as was the expression on your face.

Unaware of your intentions
still trusting I sensed no danger,
you entered my room familiar
when you left you were a stranger.

—CHRISTOPHER J. GOODEN

FOREWORD

FROM MY FIRST experience of abuse I somehow knew my life would be permanently changed. I did not know how or to what degree, but because the experience was so foreign to my existing life and completely horrific, it seemed inevitable that the change was going to be for the worse. Unable to even partially comprehend the magnitude and eventual repercussions from that horrible encounter, I instantaneously became blanketed with an overwhelming sense of shame. I can remember after my first experience, intensely feeling a sense of unworthiness. Consequently, in my mind, I immediately became damaged goods. This negative perception would become a governing force in my life. It would categorically and detrimentally impact decisions concerning family, friendships, intimate relationships, marriage, and even having children, to name a few. I was often left second-guessing myself and certainly distrusting those individuals who attempted to get close to me. Lastly, this perception created within me a mind-set filled with trepidation, so much so that when I was able to experience positive emotions regardless of the source, they would only be ephemeral or temporary. For the longest time, I never felt deserving of positive emotions or accolades. My protocol was to run from or sabotage them.

It is important to note here one of the most damning residuals from sexual abuse and the damaged goods perception is noticeably linked to sexual activity. Over the years

I have frequently seen victims, men and women, struggle with their sexuality. Many became sexually promiscuous at a very early age and helplessly lived with a constant struggle to maintain an acceptable identity without being sexual. While these are just a few of the many issues tied to sexual abuse, one can clearly see the ramifications of sexual abuse are far-reaching and intensely consuming.

When I first began to deal with my abuse, I became painfully discriminating. Only a select few could know my secret. As is the case with many victims, the overwhelming need to be accepted after sharing my secret coupled with a contrasting fear of being rejected made this process extremely difficult.

I shall remember without fail one of my first attempts to share the consuming pain of my past as I cautiously entertained a modest hope of finding comfort. One night while in college, I was sitting in my dorm room with several of my closest friends. We were at the time discussing various hardships we had encountered throughout our lives. It became quite an emotional gathering as several friends shared experiences and emotions warranting a type of bonding I had never experienced or believed possible between men. Having been privy to such an experience, I evolved a previously unachieved level of confidence that led me to stand and share my story.

There I stood in the middle of the my room, sweating from fear, with my nervous heart pounding so hard I thought it was going to burst. I remember having the feelings I used to get when I was in church and the preacher asked if anyone wanted to come down and join the church. I wanted to go down to the altar, but would always stay in my seat, thinking, "I'll go down next week." Well this time I "went down to the altar."

I attempted to transition into my story by first acknowl-edging my friends' stories and offering support to their individual pains. That process was short lived. My need and the opportunity to finally share with my friends led me to quickly delve into my story. I went straight to the heart of the matter. I was very open and honest providing very specific and graphic details of my abuse. When I finished telling my story, the room was filled with silence. Not a word was said for a few minutes. Finally one of my buddies suggested we go get something to eat and drink. I knew at that moment my story had shocked and overwhelmed them all. I knew this because the bonding and support that previously took place when others shared their stories had suddenly come to an end. No one offered me words of encouragement nor reached out to hug or comfort me even though I stood there before them with tears running from my eyes. We ended up leaving my room. As we left everyone went ahead of me. I can remember riding to the store with dead silence in the car. I can also remember at that very moment, regretting sharing my story.

The next morning several of my buddies came to get me and took me to breakfast. I imagine they talked amongst themselves and decided it might be a good idea to come check on me. I was grateful that they did. We went and had a good time at breakfast. But it was as though I had not even told them about my story. No one mentioned my conversa-tion. To this day out of the six men in that room, only one has demonstrated the courage over the past twenty years to ask me about my experience.

Now, these facts notwithstanding, this is not an indict-ment of my friends or a slight toward them. I still maintain quality relationships with these gentlemen and consider them all to be extended family members. They are all like brothers. Before going any further, let me mention that I have had similar responses from the females I have shared my experiences with. I believe all of my male and female friends wanted to reach out to me. The painful part for me was that they simply did not know how.

To add insight to this dilemma, allow me to briefly share my first encounter with a trained professional in counseling. I was referred to a psychologist while in college because I consistently exhibited a level of anger determined to be detrimental to myself and others. After a couple of sessions it became apparent to my therapist my issues were very serious. Prompted by several direct questions as to the source of my anger, I eventually confided that I was raped when I was a child. He immediately became enraged and told me we would assess my anger in our next session.

When I arrived at my next session, my therapist had carefully placed four chairs in the middle of the room. There were the two chairs we sat in and two chairs placed in front of us. Resting in one of the empty chairs was a stick about eighteen inches long, covered with a foamed pad. The padding was about ten inches long and five inches in diameter. After we took a seat I asked my therapist, "Why are there two empty seats?" To make a long story short, he asked me to pretend the people who abused me were sitting in the chairs in front of me. My challenge was to confront them. I tried harnessing my true emotions and sat there talking to two make believe people. After some intense probing from my therapist as to my true feelings, I erupted with unbridled anger and reckless abandon. With that padded stick in my hand, I tore that office apart. When I turned around my therapist was standing in the corner of the office looking at me with great fear, with his hands up as if to protect himself. I knew at that time I needed some help. The discouraging thing was however, that my therapist said he did know if he could help me. After a long discussion he decided to see me for an undetermined number of sessions. I guess he felt like my friends did in that he did not know how to help me. But thanks be to God, this therapist became a springboard to my healing.

I have shared these stories because they speak to the very core of the managing problem victims of abuse have to confront. The very nature of our pain requires an unyielding resolve and constant access to individuals who have and are willing to offer a supreme level of understanding, compassion, and support. I believe there are many people who can do the latter, but for whatever reason, many people seem to wrongly feel inept with regard to their ability to help. The sad thing here is that simply offering to listen can be so therapeutic for victims. But rather than try, many potential supporters choose to keep their distance, leaving us regrettably to fight this difficult battle on our own.

When I became a victim of sexual abuse, it was as though I was convicted of a crime. A crime someone else committed and for which it was I who was then wrongly imprisoned. While I was not physically locked away in a prison cell, the majority of my life has been spent in an emotional prison. It was the internalization of so many negative emotions from my abuse coupled with the "guards" I created to protect myself that kept me imprisoned. Like many of the innocent men and women who have been imprisoned for crimes they did not commit, I have had to live my life defending myself. I tried so desperately to find someone to believe me, someone to understand my emotions, someone to help set me free, and someone to understand that I was an innocent child when this happened to me. Most importantly, I had to find someone who understood that because I wanted and needed to tell my story so I could heal, I was not committing a crime by doing so.

There exists a sad state of affairs for victims of sexual abuse. This has led me to develop what is slowly becoming an inalterable conclusion with regard to attitudes toward victims of sexual abuse. The terrible crime committed against us, because of its very fowl and disgusting nature, leaves us with a stigma entirely associated with that of a rape victim. There are always suspicious questions concerning how and why and a prevailing belief that these matters should not become public. As a result, little sensitivity, compassion, or consideration is given to the very real fact that no woman or child wants or deserves to have the core of their exis-tence, their heart and spirit, tragically taken away in such a vile, depraved, and vicious manner. When you are left feeling *judged for a crime committed against you*, it becomes extremely difficult to overcome the internalized feeling of being damaged goods.

The clear absence of consistent and productive support systems makes it appear that victims of sexual abuse are all alone and not many people care about us. It is as though we suffer from leprosy and no one wants to be near us. When we seek help, the most common response is to cast us off somewhere and not talk about this horrible crime. Sadly, this incomprehensible attitude has thereby allowed this horrible crime to continuously and regrettably impact the lives of millions of innocent children. As a result, many of these same children become adult victims living their lives with walls or "guards" around their hearts, utterly unable to live emotionally healthy and productive lives.

I have lived the majority of my life emotionally imprisoned by the scars from my abuse. As a result, I developed very debilitating "guards" or coping mechanisms that I thought were protecting me. The heartbreaking truth is that they were only hindering my growth and certainly preventing my heart from healing. These guards were also responsible for what I believe to be the greatest injustice of this crime, a lingering inability to love and receive love.

This story is about my abuse and how it impacted my life. It is about how God intervened in my life and transformed me. This is my testimony of how a power greater than me, God, rescued me from the depths of a great despair and a life of extreme violence. It is about how God helped me to overcome the very guards I developed out of a need to protect my heart, how He showed me these guards were destroying my life, and how He helped me to release these guards so that my heart could heal. This story is about how I had to learn to replace my guards of anger, pandemonium, pride, bitterness, and hatred with peace, humility, kindness, acceptance, and most importantly, love.

I am not professing to be perfect. But I am professing to be a changed man, albeit with the help of God. I still have room for growth. And as I will discuss, I am likened to a recovering alcoholic. Just like I engaged in negative behaviors that were destroying my life, I had to make a conscious decision to learn and engage in positive behaviors that would enhance my life. Like the recovering alcoholic I had to learn to surround myself with people who knew my plight, people and activities that supported my need for change, and I had to constantly remind myself of where I was and came from, so I could concentrate on where I wanted to be.

To those who read this story and are victims of abuse, it is my desire to offer you a lasting hope and belief in God, such that you too can overcome the hurt and pain from your abuse. To those who read this story and are not victims but may know someone who has been victimized, it is my hope that you will gain insight and a better understanding of the plight of your friends and loved ones. My story is a reminder to all, that unless we stand up and protect our innocent and defenseless children, countless more will fall victim to this senseless atrocity, many of whom will be victimized inexcusably, while you are reading this text.

Before giving way to the story, allow me to make a final point. After completing this book, I was asked, "Why would you write about this and how would it affect your family?" My response was simply this, "When I was sexually abused, my innocence, my dignity, and my faith in others were immediately stripped from me. The person I was prior to my abuse, died. I have had to mourn the loss of parts of my identity that I can never get back. I have also had to evolve into someone with a reason to live and a will to love. If this is not a terrible crime and injustice, I do not know what is. I have a right...and an obligation to bring to the forefront as much information as I can to help other victims of sexual abuse."

This is my sincere effort to assist in ending this horrible crime. As you read this story, open your heart not to me, but to the countless children and adult victims of this horrendous crime who have yet to heal.

To God be the glory.

Chapter 1

MY CHILDHOOD

A S I PREPARED to tell my story, I began to reflect on my life and my experiences. While doing so, it became very obvious I had many memories from every part of my life, except my childhood. I understand now that a lot of my memories were blocked as a result of my abuse. To that end I am deeply saddened that I know or remember so little about such an integral part of my life. It is difficult accepting that a part of my development and who I am are missing from my memory. I can remember as an adult sitting with friends listening to them share their many childhood experiences as they laughed and smiled while talking about their siblings and relationships with their parents. I can also remember always just sitting there, silent, because I could not remember any stories worthy of sharing. With this in mind, here are the best recollections of my early childhood.

I was born at Fort Campbell, Kentucky, October 24, 1958. I was the sixth of eight children. My family consists of four boys and four girls. I have three older brothers, two older sisters, and two younger sisters. My father was in the army and my mother was a housewife.

As best I can remember, my family moved around a lot because my father was in the military. I remember stories about how we went back and forth living in Germany and

Kentucky, both before and after I was born. I do remember my mother telling me a story about how a hot iron fell on me when we were living in Germany. I still have that scar today.

We lived in Kentucky until I was seven years old. During that time my two younger sisters were born, one during another of my father's tours in Germany and the other when we returned to Kentucky.

I remember spending most of my time interacting with my siblings. With eight children in the home there was always something to do. Needless to say, they became my closest friends, especially my brothers. I spent most of my time outside of school around my brothers. I am quite sure a lot of that time was to their regret. My two oldest brothers were my heroes. They were good athletes, they could fight, and since I was such a small child, they were big men in my eyes. They were the protectors of my family. No one wanted to mess with the "Gooden boys."

Because we had so many children, my father always worked several jobs after his army duties ended. He would work late into the night so I would often be in bed by the time he got home. I do not have many memories from my interactions with him.

My father was a serious man. We all tried our best not to make him mad because he did not have a problem disciplining us. He gave the worst whippings. I learned a lot of my lessons as a child about what to do and not to do from the whippings my father gave my siblings. Having witnessed their mistakes, I learned early how to keep in line.

My mother was our sole supporter with regard to school and any other activities we were involved in. I do not remember us being allowed to participate in too many activities outside of school because we had so many children and it was too costly. Consequently, a great emphasis was placed on performing well in school. School was always a fun place for me. I did get picked on a lot by other kids because I was always small for my age. Outside of that, as best I can remember, school was an enjoyable place to be.

When we left Kentucky we moved to Cleveland, Ohio, because my father had to go to Vietnam. My father chose Ohio for us to live because he had two brothers living there who would look out for our family. We lived in Ohio for a year. That was how long my father had to stay in Vietnam.

We lived in the projects while we were in Ohio. Even though it was obvious we were not rich, my mother taught us to appreciate what we had and we really did not want for anything. One of my fondest memories from living in Ohio and as a kid occurred one Sunday after church. Before leaving for church that morning my mother prepared some meatloaf for dinner. I was not a big meatloaf fan. She left it sitting in the oven for us to eat when we returned home. Much to our surprise, when we returned home and my mother opened the oven there were rats eating our dinner. We were somewhat disappointed and hungry, but not so much for the meatloaf. My mom loaded up the car and said we will have to eat out. I remember us passing some restaurant called "The Golden Arches." I pointed at it and said, "What's that place, Mom?" She said, "I don't know son, but we're going to try it." This was my first time ever eating at a McDonalds and I have not been the same since. I do not think there was a happier kid on the earth that day. I never knew a cheeseburger and fries could taste so good.

Our neighborhood was filled with poor whites, blacks, and Hispanics. I can remember developing different feelings about other races while in Ohio. When we were in Kentucky, it was not uncommon to be reminded we were black. Most of my friends at school and at home were black. The "N-word" was used a lot. But things were a little different in Ohio. Since everyone was poor, no one thought they were better than anyone else. I guess someone determined it would best if we all just got along and we did. I do not remember being picked on very much when we lived in Ohio. I do remember being in one fight, but that was all. As I mentioned earlier, everyone seemed to get along.

I was also able to develop great relationships with my cousins while living in Ohio. We would have sleepovers and for me it was like having two more sisters and one more brother. Because of them we were able to do more things socially like going to amusement parks or to the movies, because my uncles and aunts would help out financially.

As best I can remember I was a pretty happy kid up to that point. By then I had become quite shy, which mainly had to do with my physical size. Because I was so small, most people intimidated me. I also developed an appreciation for school. That was the one place I knew I could always make my mother proud of me. Her approval meant the world to me. Lastly, I developed a strong sense of family. Because we did so much together and depended on each other for so many things, my family was pretty much my entire world. As long as everyone in the house was happy, I was happy, too.

There were always clear constants in my life. Family was made a priority, performing well in school was extremely important, and my mother made sure we attended Sunday school and church as often as we could. We did not spend a lot of time talking about God, but I knew He was important to my mother and she wanted God to be an integral part of our lives.

I remember the excitement and joy my uncles, aunts, and especially my mother showed when my father returned from Vietnam. My siblings were also glad my father was back. We all missed him, but another reality was that we were more than ready to get out of the projects and move somewhere else.

I never really understood why my father had to leave us and go to war. I never asked, either. I simply thought it was something everyone's father did so I adjusted accordingly. And because I never really developed a close relationship with my father before he left, I guess the adjustment was made somewhat easier. That night when all the celebrating began I was blown away by all the emotions and excitement. I remember joining in on the celebrations, but at the same time being completely confused. I sat there thinking to myself, "How can people be so happy and spend so much time crying at the same time?"

When we left Ohio we took a short vacation and eventually moved to Fayetteville, North Carolina, where my life would be changed forever.

Chapter 2

FAMILIAR STRANGER

I AM NOT QUITE sure how or why things began to happen to me. I will never be able to understand that. But I am very sure of the horrible things that took place in my bedroom. While I did not know what was going on or what to call it, I was always left with a sick feeling and a guarded belief within my heart that it was very wrong. I was not sure if I was the only one doing something wrong, which may have elicited some measure of guilt on my part, or if everyone involved was doing something wrong. I just knew it felt terribly wrong!

The frightening and haunting memories from those events were forever etched in my heart and mind, primarily because of the extreme physical and foul nature of the abuse, and equally because of the overwhelming sense of helplessness I felt each and every night I was abused. At the age of nine I was a very small kid. It is doubtful that I weighed sixty pounds at the time, probably the same weight of a lot of kids in lower grades. I tell myself I must have been very small at that age. When I entered high school I weighed a whopping ninety-two pounds. I did put on some weight that year. I was a member of the wrestling team my ninth grade year and wrestled at the ninety-eight-pound weight class at the age of fourteen.

While I have clear and vivid memories from many of the

nights I was molested, I do realize there were also many nights I either consciously or unconsciously blocked out of my memory. Things began to happen so frequently I remember at times feeling completely numb to the experiences, as if I were just some type of puppet being manipulated in a show. Nonetheless, I will always remember the first time I was molested and I will always remember the last attempt my abusers made to molest me.

I will always remember the first night I was molested because it was a typical night that turned so crazy so quickly. We were living in Hammond Hills, a neighborhood on Fort Bragg Army base in Fayetteville, North Carolina. As one of the youngest of eight children it was not uncommon for me and my two younger sisters to have to go to bed before everyone else. We would go through our usual routine of playing around which generally led to someone coming upstairs to check on us and make sure we were finally in the bed. This was the case whether it was just family at home or if we had company. This particular night I remember being yelled at from downstairs to "Go to bed!" I knew this meant there would soon be someone coming upstairs to check on us. True to form, someone did come upstairs. I remember giggling as I rushed to crawl under my covers as I tried to listen for the footsteps of someone coming to my room. Because this was such a common occurrence, I began laughing as the door opened because I knew, or at least I thought I knew, I would be chastised and told to go to sleep.

This night, however, was completely different. When the door opened, it was a male relative. He turned on the lights and in a manner completely different from what I was expecting he put his hands to his lips and whispered for me to be quiet and come from under the covers. Since I had no reason to be suspicious I did as I was told. But as soon as I came from under the covers, he turned the lights out and sat in the bed with me. I asked him why he turned the lights off to which he replied we are going to play a game. As an option to going to bed, I quickly chose to play a game. The game consisted of him touching and tickling me for a while. I was also asked to tickle and touch him back. However, the game did not last long, as he finally grabbed my hand and told me to touch something. I could not see what it was, but I knew it felt very strange to me. I remember pulling away saying "No, that's nasty!" Shortly after this point, I remember him pulling my arms above my head and binding them. He pulled my pajamas down from my legs, muzzled my mouth, and raped me. I am not sure how long the experience lasted, but I do know it seemed like it lasted forever. After raping me, this relative left the room, but not before telling me he would "kill me" if I told anyone what happened. This experience left me entirely overwhelmed as my perpetrator was someone who used to protect me. He was a hero in my mind. This person who was once so *familiar* to me had now became a complete *stranger.*

Left physically in pain, completely beleaguered, and confused, I laid in the bed until one of my older brothers came to bed. I was laying there crying and shaking under my blankets, afraid to let him know what had just happened to me. As best I could, I tried to pretend I was asleep. I do not recall getting much sleep that night, as there was a constant feeling of something running down my behind between my legs. Before anyone could get into the bathroom the next morning, I jumped in the shower and tried with all my might to cleanse my body from the horrible pain I was feeling.

For the first couple of weeks these horrible events took place several times a week. The anxiety about having to go to bed at night was overwhelming. I remember getting into trouble at school for falling asleep in class and for not doing my schoolwork. As if this was not bad enough, there came a night when two of my male relatives came to my room. They both molested me and I was humiliated even more as I was passed between the two men like a piece of meat. One watched while the other took his turn. And as was always the case, I was left trembling from physical pain and in fear for my life. They repeatedly told me they would "kill me" if I told anyone else.

The very nature of these experiences became more disgusting as time went on. I was forced to perform other acts. As always I was left to deal with the degrading feeling of something dripping down my legs afterward.

Somehow, time passed and I managed to get promoted to the fourth grade. Over the course of that year, I am not quite sure when, I someway began developing a stronger resolve each time I was molested. I know I became meaner with my siblings and peers at school. Some people commented on my changes, but still I was unable to explain them. I can remember getting to the point when I would resist being molested. Even though this tended to make the experience even more painful, as I would be beaten up as well, I derived some sort of satisfaction knowing I had some kind of fighter instinct within me. I told myself that if it was going to happen, then I was going to do my part to resist. I had adopted the belief that what they were doing to me was completely wrong and even though I had no idea when,

I knew it had to stop and I wanted and needed it to stop immediately!

The last night an attempt was made to molest me, I made up in my mind before going to bed that I had had enough. I spent a good amount of energy strategizing as to how I could end this horrible crime. Unable to come up with any clear plan, I just decided within my heart that enough was enough and I was not going to take it anymore. So that night when they came to molest me, I jumped out of the bed and started swinging at them and punching them as hard as I possibly could. I also yelled at them, saying, "You shouldn't be doing these things!" and "I will tell if you do it anymore!" Lastly I looked at both of them with tears in my eyes and told them if they ever touched me again I would kill them. Was this some kind of sick or ironic form of poetic justice?

That ended my year of molestation. While I was truly grateful it was over, I had already begun to feel the repercussions of what I had experienced over the past year. My life was to be forever changed. I had already begun to feel the onset of a developing self-hatred, a terrible self-esteem, and a propensity to become enraged and physical at the drop of a hat. And just as one horrible set of events came to an end, a more intense and punishing set of circumstances began to unfold.

I was now left to begin the seemingly impossible task of accepting and dealing with what had happened to me. Managing my emotions, which were all over the place, was already a difficult task. Keeping secret the shameful nature of my life was a must, as well as trying to maintain some form of loyalty to my family. Finally finding a way to somehow believe I was not responsible for what happened to me had become extremely important. Absolving myself from any guilt or sense of responsibility for what happened was critical if I were ever to feel as though I could and would someday be whole again.

Chapter 3

IN JAIL: MY JOSEPH EXPERIENCE

I N THE BOOK of Genesis the story of Joseph is used to demonstrate how God will take what the enemy intended for harm and turn it to good. Joseph was the youngest and most favored son of his father, Israel. He often had dreams he would share with his brothers and father of how he would be raised up throughout the land and become a leader over many people. Because he was the youngest of twelve brothers, these dreams often generated resentment from his older brothers especially when his father rebuked Joseph, but still entertained Joseph's dreams. They thought Joseph was presumptuous and hated the thought that he was implying they would someday bow down and worship their younger brother.

Over time Joseph's brothers developed a great hatred for him. As a result, when an opportunity presented itself they plotted to kill Joseph. When the time came to implement their plan they decided not to kill Joseph and sold him into slavery.

While Joseph was in slavery he was thrown into jail in Egypt. An Egyptian who was one of Pharaoh's officials later bought him. While at the home of his new master, God showed Joseph great favor and blessed everything he did for his master thereby allowing his new master to prosper mightily. As a result, Joseph was given complete reign over his master's affairs. Eventually Joseph was again faced with a plot that could ultimately do him great harm. His master's wife tried to get Joseph to sleep with her and when her plot failed, she lied to her husband only to have Joseph thrown in prison again. The Lord again showed Joseph great favor and while in prison used him to interpret dreams for Pharaoh's cupbearer and baker. These interpretations would come true and after two years thereby lead Pharaoh to have Joseph released from prison to interpret his own dreams. As Joseph had done with the cupbearer and baker, Joseph interpreted Pharaoh's dreams. He informed Pharaoh that seven years of prosperity and famine were to befall the land. Impressed by Joseph's knowledge, Pharaoh then put Joseph in charge of all of Egypt's affairs. He was brought into the kingdom and was to oversee plans to store enough food and grain to last throughout the famine.

When the famine came, people from all nations were forced to come to Egypt because they had not prepared for the famine. It was no coincidence that Joseph's brothers would also be sent to Egypt to request food and grain to take back to their father's home. They were unaware however, that Joseph was now the great ruler he spoke of in his dreams. After two meetings with his brothers, Joseph finally revealed himself to them. His brothers were filled with guilt and sorrow and repented.

Joseph now understood God's plan for his life and informed his brothers that it was not them who sold him into slavery. He told them God allowed for him to be sold into slavery so His will could be done. Joseph was to save Egypt from famine and destruction and under his governing Egypt was to become a very prosperous nation. Joseph forgave his brothers and showed them how God took what the enemy intended for harm and turned it into good.

It was not my intention to go into such detail with this story. But for the purpose of this and later chapters the essence of this story had to be shared.

While I did not experience the great physical challenges of going to jail as Joseph did, my "in-jail" experiences were clearly physical and I dare say more emotional for me. Each time my abusers left me, it felt as though I was being left alone to die a slow death emotionally and spiritually. I often wished I would die during the experiences and clearly wished I were dead afterward. The effects from this abuse were so traumatizing that there were times as a child and as an adult when I did contemplate ending my or my abusers' lives.

It became very clear over time, that all my abusers could see and were concerned about was fulfilling their own sick and selfish needs. When Joseph's brothers became fed up and wanted him out of the way, they did not give any consideration to how Joseph might fair as a slave and clearly did not give any consideration as to how this would affect their father or their family. Like Joseph's brothers, my abusers were also selfishly motivated. Just as Joseph's brothers did not consider the fact that they could have been caught or any other consequences, my abusers appeared to give no thought to their behavior or possible consequences. The boldness and frequency with which they abused me was and still is mind-boggling. Not only was it clear they were not concerned about themselves, this was clearly taking place without concern for how their actions might impact me or my family.

Each experience drained me to my core as I would be left completely exhausted. During the time of the abuse, I never felt the experiences were something I would ever be able to physically or emotionally recover from. Left with so many questions, I never saw a light at the beginning of the tunnel let alone a light at the end of the tunnel. I can imagine Joseph feeling that same kind of despair as he was sold into slavery. It was this rapidly growing belief that sent me spiraling emotionally and led to the development of so many of my negative defense mechanisms which became the "guards" protecting my significantly wounded heart.

I wish to note here that my relationship with God has not always existed as it should in my heart and mind. But I thank God that just as He was always with Joseph during his journey, it has become very obvious that God has had His hands on my life for a long, long time. I am reminded of the *Footprints* poem and the verse when God is asked, "Why was there a time when there were only one set of footprints?" To which God replied, "There was only one set of footprints at that time because that is when I was carrying you." This is how I see my life. But for me there have been many times on my journey when there was only one set of footprints. God had to step in and protect me not only from the enemy, but He also protected me from myself.

Chapter 4

GET UP AND WALK: MY
POOL OF BETHESDA

WHILE JESUS WAS teaching in Jerusalem He stopped at a pool named Bethesda. This was a place where "the blind, the lame, and the paralyzed" would go to wash themselves (John 5:3). It was a common belief that if they were able to be washed in the pool when the water was "stirring," they would be healed of their illnesses. There was one man, an invalid, who had been coming to the pool for some thirty-eight years. This same man, however, was never able to get in the pool, because no one would help him get in and he clearly was unable to get into the pool by himself.

When Jesus arrived at the pool and was told about the invalid, he went to the man to discuss his plight. Historians say that Jesus asked the man three separate times, "Do you want to be healed?" (John 5:6). The first two times the man offered several excuses saying he could not get into the pool by himself, no one was willing to help him get into the pool, and that when the water was stirring people would push him out of the way and go before him.

Impressed by the man's faith in the healing powers of the pool, Jesus asked the man a third time, "Do you want to be healed?" The man replied yes. Jesus then said to the man, "Get up! Pick up your mat and walk" (John 5:8–9). At that moment the man was healed. He picked up his mat and walked away.

This story is critical to my own. Not knowing fully the consequences of my actions, I spent thirty-one years waddling in my own self-pity. I took time to blame everyone else for what happened to me as a child and I also made time to clearly blame everyone else for my not being healed. I blamed my family, my abusers for not coming forward themselves, and I blamed those friends I told about my abuse, as I felt they did not offer the kind of support I felt I needed and deserved.

I spent so much time over these years trying to find ways to protect myself. As a result, I built walls around my heart that I thought were impenetrable. These walls were composed of anger, pride, hatred, and pity, to name a few. These same walls eventually became, in my mind, like guards surrounding a fort with the fort representing my heart. I was determined to never be hurt again. No one was going to get close enough to hurt me emotionally or physically again.

Compounding the issues that came with these walls, I also developed a sense of denial. For years I spent an inordinate amount of time and energy trying to develop an alter ego; a person I could be proud of, and more importantly a person other people would be proud of. I tried to turn myself into something and someone I was not.

I can remember not too long after my abuse searching for ways to feel good about myself. I would throw myself into my schoolwork doing all I could to outperform my classmates. I believed by doing so, this would some how ease some of the pain and shame I was still feeling from my abuse. I also got into sports. I participated in as many different sports as I could. I played basketball, baseball, and football. I learned how to shoot pool at a high level, eventually getting to the point where I won several tournaments. I mastered table tennis and bowling and played in semi-pro leagues in both sports. I became astute in board games such as chess. I became a card whiz. I learned how to ice skate. I studied martial arts. I became an excellent swimmer, and I lifted weights. All of these were attempts to give me some sense of pride about myself. For a while my successes in each of these areas offered me some superficial pride and temporarily boosted my self-esteem. But no matter what I did or what I was able to accomplish, the guards that were surrounding my heart—my pride, anger, hatred, and pity—would not allow any type of positive emotions to stay inside my heart for long. I was left searching for more ways to boost my self-esteem. I was still an abused child who was turning into an abused adult who had not been healed.

Over the years so much of my existence became contingent on meeting the approval of others. It is ironic to note here that some of the very things I did to try and improve my self-esteem were the very things that I admired in my abusers. As I mentioned earlier, over time I developed a sick sense of loyalty to my abusers. I felt more obligated to protect them and our secret than I did myself. When I had an opportunity I tried with all my might to emulate them. So in some strange way in the midst of my confusion, I maintained a twisted desire to even impress the very persons who sent me spiraling down this road. Again similar to my abusers, I took it upon myself to become a "lady's man." While I was not as promiscuous as a lot of my male friends, I was very active. I can remember sitting down one day telling myself I was going to sleep with as many women as possible. This was to serve three purposes. First, it was going to make me look good before my peers. Secondly, it was a means for me to dole out some form of punishment. I had gotten to the point in my life where as long as I was feeling pain I was going to make others feel pain. I hurt many young ladies during this phase of my life. I can only thank God for His forgiveness and mercy. Lastly, this behavior was to serve as some kind of confirmation. Having been sexually abused, I wondered at times if I were going to become a homosexual. There were several times during my life when I was approached by gay men, which triggered these thoughts and sent me into a rage. So again, it was extremely important to have my sexuality validated by being with as many women as possible.

I tried many other things to make me feel good about myself and to take my mind off my real issues. I became a borderline alcoholic and I also became a very frequent user of marijuana. I sought out these activities to keep my mind off my pain. They were an attempt to at least dull the pain a little. These proved to be very negative forces in my life.

After graduating from college it was not uncommon for me to drink four to five days a week. And I drank heavily. Some form of violent outburst typically followed my drinking. I had to be taken to the doctor once because I literally went through a window after a man. Fortunately, I did not do any serious harm to him or myself, but I do still have a notice-able scar from this event.

I also remember with much regret a very unfortunate inci-dent that took place in my apartment. I had some friends over one night and we were drinking and smoking. One thing led to another and one of my friends began to antagonize me. I had at the time sitting in the corner of my living room a cast iron spear about five feet long that my brother brought me from Africa. As my friend continued to taunt me I believe he came to realize he might need to leave. When he got to the door I picked the spear up and hurled it at him. It went through his shirt and stuck in the door. It was nothing more than the grace of God that saved me from harpooning and killing that man.

This type of aggressive behavior became frequent. There were even times, especially on the weekends, when I could feel myself getting "roused up" from drinking when I would handcuff myself to my heater and throw the key across the room. I would then call someone to come over the next day and let me out. It is sad that I would begin drinking with the mind-set that I might have to do something so extreme to protect myself and others. But again this is how far I had to go to try and numb my pain.

While these events clearly demonstrated the depth of my pain and lack of self-control, three of my most horrible and frightening experiences took place while I was under the influence of alcohol and marijuana. As I mentioned earlier, one of my guards was anger. I used my anger as often as I could as a means to keep people away from me. I have had many violent outbursts in my life and I do not have the time to detail all of the fights I was involved in. But two fights stick out in my mind very readily that detail the pain I was in, the fact that I wanted someone else to feel my pain, and most importantly, that I was so much into my pity party that I did not even care about my own well-being. A third incident which is truly significant also details the fears that were still embracing my heart. All of these incidents occurred while I was in college, which was a time of my life where my pity party was at an all-time high.

One night I was watching the door at a fraternity party when a man came up and grabbed the money. I had been drinking a lot that night so my energy level was very high. He took off running out of the building. My friends and I quickly followed. When we caught up with the man I took it upon myself to confront him. Here again I was trying to bolster my image before my peers. The confrontation took a turn for the worse almost immediately. The man and I began fighting and I remember so vividly telling myself I was going to kill this man. I had him down on the ground and began to choke him with my bare hands. In my mind I had already processed how I was going to continue clasping my fingers around his neck until there was no more room. His neck was to disappear within my fingers and I was not going to stop until he forfeited his final breath. It was by nothing but the grace of God this unfortunate incident was stopped. During the brawl several of my friends tried to pull me off this man. I remember hearing them yelling and screaming my name saying, "Stop! You're going to kill him!" And as I looked around at them, I remember the sick calmness I had as I believed what I was doing was justified and needed to be finished. With this man gasping for air and begging for help, one of my closest friends came over and whispered my name in my ear. Like a savage dog that had been called off of a kill by a whistle from his master, I immediately let go of the man's neck and rolled over on the ground. As I looked at my peers and throughout the crowd, I was embarrassed and frightened by the fact that I almost killed a man over a few dollars. I also felt a great pain as I knew this man was paying for my past. This again was clearly an example of the state of pity I was in and demonstrated how much I wanted someone, anyone, to feel like I was feeling.

The second incident occurred one night when I was returning to my dormitory from a ball with my girlfriend.

I had been drinking, but not a lot. We were approached on the elevator by two white students who abruptly called us "n——s." I became outraged, but because my girlfriend was with me, I knew I had to get her back to the room before I could do anything.

After getting her to the room, I quickly ran out to try and find the guys we ran into. And much to my surprise, I did. I immediately chased them down and followed them to their suite. I began banging on their door, yelling and screaming for them to "Come on out and fight this n——r!" The level of rage I was experiencing had me again convinced I was justified to exact a great deal of harm and pain to these men. After five to ten minutes of acting like a crazed fool in the hallway, one of the guys opened his door. I will always remember the expression on his face when he opened the door. He stood there with a grin on his face as he held a butcher knife in his hand that I am sure was at least ten to twelve inches long. He then said to me, "What do you want to do n——r?" Without thinking I jumped on the man. He swung the knife at me and fortunately for me he missed. With the amount of rage I had in me, the fight did not last long. I left him there on the floor crying for help.

This incident again is memorable for me because it is one of the first times I realized just how much pain I was in. It was very stupid of me to chase those guys down. It was even more stupid for me to jump on a man wielding a knife before me when I had no means of protecting myself. I was filled with so much hatred and pain that it did not even cross my mind that I could have been killed during that fight. The truth be known, even if I had thought about it, I probably would have still jumped on the man. That is how devastating my pity party had become.

The final incident occurred one night while I was hanging out with a bunch of my friends. As was the case for us on a Friday night, we had been drinking pretty heavily when we were approached by the campus police. Things got out of control very fast and we were told emphatically if we did not leave we were going to be arrested. One of my friends got in one officer's face and began to argue with him, accusing him of being racist. Again having a desire to bolster my ego and show off before my peers, I pushed my friend aside and immediately began to disrespect the officer. One thing led to another and I was quickly arrested and thrown in the back of a police car.

As we drove off, the seriousness of the events quickly hit me and I begged to no avail for the officers to let me go. I apologized and promised they would never have to see me again. My efforts were in vain. During the ride to the police station, the officers began to taunt me saying, "Yea, you're not a big shot now, are you?" A few other things were said and the bottom line was they had succeeded in scaring the living daylights out of me. When we got to the police station I again begged for them to let me go. My begging did me no good. I so desperately did not want to go to jail. It had always been one of my deepest fears.

I was processed into the jail and allowed to make my one phone call. Fortunately I was able to get my friends and they assured me they would be down to the station to bail me out. Just as they were preparing to give me my jumpsuit, an officer came in and said my bail was posted. I cannot describe the relief I felt at that moment.

When I got in the car with my friends they began to laugh and joke. But I was not able to join in on the fun. We made it back to the dormitory and as we got out of the car,

I leaned over on one of my friends and began to cry like a baby. While this appeared completely strange to them, since I was such a tough guy, I knew in my heart what my tears were for. The only thing I could think about on the way to the jail was that I did not want to be locked up with a bunch of men. I was beginning to think that my worst fear might come true again. That fear was that I was going to be raped in jail. I could not handle the thought of experiencing that again, especially as an adult.

Prior to these incidents, I had been involved in counseling periodically. As I mentioned earlier, I had truly convinced myself that I had healed to some degree. I ended up back in counseling after this last event. This was certainly the most intensive counseling I had ever experienced. It proved to be very helpful, as I did not have many more crazy episodes in college. Nonetheless, I continued to be involved in similar activities from my late twenties to my mid thirties. Counseling continued to help when I occasionally started to get out of control. I would still, however, continue my cycle of substance abuse, which dominated my personality. Promiscuity and violence were mainstays with me.

I continued during this time, as I always had, to develop my relationship with the Lord. I would take two steps forward spiritually and one step backward. It was not until my mid thirties when I developed some form of resolve spiritually that I began to recognize my need for a consistent walk with the Lord. It had become painfully obvious that I needed the kind of help I could not give myself and the kind of help no other person could give me. This was made more evident when two of my closest friends in the matter of six months apart approached me saying they were grateful for my relationship with the Lord. I asked both of them why they were so concerned and they both gave me the same answer. They both said their biggest fear for me when we were in college was that I was going to end up in prison because I had killed someone. I asked them both if they were so worried about me why they did not confront me then. They again had the same answer. They said I was so far gone emotionally they did not think I would listen to them and they were also afraid of me.

As I continued to pursue my relationship with the Lord, it became clear to me that I desperately needed to deal with the abuse from my childhood. The time had come for me to take this task head on. Looking back now I can see how and where the Lord offered me hope and healing through my friends and even through the counseling. I just ignored it and continued with my pity party. I was comfortable there. I did not begin to experience a release until the time I spoke at my church and was reminded of the pool of Bethesda experience and how it was time for me to pick up my mat, come out of my pity party, and take responsibility for my healing. The Lord asked me if I was finally ready to be healed. I finally said yes after thirty-one years.

I can see now where and how the Lord offered to help me heal from my pain. He was very specific with regard to how and why He wanted to help me. He was offering me a chance to develop and strengthen a personal relationship with Him.

So after all of my running, after all of my blaming everyone else for my pain and lack of healing, after all of the pain I caused others both physically and emotionally, after all the help the Lord offered me through counseling and friends, after all of my excuses, after all the times the Lord protected me from webs of self-destruction, after all of the alcohol and marijuana I consumed, after all the times the Lord protected me from being hurt or from hurting someone else, and after all of my messing around, the Lord continued to pursue me and offer me help. It was not until January of 1998 when the Lord reminded me of the Bethesda experience—and I decided, yes, I did want to heal, and yes, I knew my healing would come to pass through my relationship with the Lord under His guidance. I have lived a very challenging life. But praise be to God, the Source of my strength and my Deliverer, I am still standing.

Chapter 5

STANDING IN AGREEMENT

I HAVE ALWAYS BEEN amazed by the perceptions and feedback from others when I told them I wanted to go to my family and talk about my abuse. I was often asked, "Why do you want to do that? Can't you see the harm it's going to do to your mother and your family?" To which I would reply, "What about the damage that has been done to me?" I would then be told, "Since you've dealt with it for this long, why can't you let it go?" I replied, "I want and need to be healed because the memories and pain are destroying my life!"

Sadly this is a dilemma most victims of sexual abuse have to face. As a result, it creates a set of circumstances wherein we are "damned if we do and damned if we don't." By this I mean if we choose to keep quiet, we cannot completely heal. If we talk about our story, we run the risk of being ridiculed and even hated for standing up for something we have every right to stand up for. As sad as these circumstances are, the reality is that everyone should be standing up for victims of sexual abuse. Everyone should also be standing up to prevent the continuation of this evil. But as long as most people choose to believe this horrible crime does not exist, or that we should not talk about it or simply choose to ignore it, this horrendous crime will never go away. As a result, many children even at this very moment will continue to be sexually abused.

The Word of God tells us in John 10:10 Jesus came, "That they may have life, and have it to the full." My interpretation of this is that God desires we live productive and happy lives. We also have the right not to have our lives destroyed by the reprehensible actions of others. But when that does happen, we also have a right to be made whole from our tragedies.

As I mentioned in my Introduction, I knew from the onset there was something terribly wrong with what was happening to me. It was this conviction, which continued to grow, that allowed me to stop the abuse and led me to fight the good fight so I could begin my path to healing. This conviction was and still is the foundation for my healing. You see in order to fight against something we must have a firm belief in ourselves and that against which we fight. While I was young, my belief was based on strong feelings within my heart. As an adult, my belief is based on the Word of God. This is important; in order for me to move forward with healing, one of the first things I had to do was stand in agreement with God. I had to acknowledge this horrible crime is wrong. Not only did I have a right to reveal it, I had an even greater right to heal.

There are many references in the Bible where God specifically addresses the expectation for parents to protect children. Sexual immorality is also addressed. It is made very clear that God is angered when children are not protected and when sexual immorality takes place. It is this same anger over such things that we have a right to share in because, again, the behavior is wrong.

Matthew 18:6 states "But if anyone causes one of these little ones who believe in me to sin, it would be better for him to have a large millstone hung around his neck and to be drowned in the depths of the sea." This scripture speaks to God's expectation that children are to be protected and not led down paths of destruction. In the Book of Leviticus chapter 18, sexual immorality and unlawful sexual relations are discussed. More specifically and for the purpose of this text, incest as it related to father-daughter relationships, mother and son relationships, and brother and sister relationships are all clearly identified as sin. Incest is also addressed in 1 Corinthians. In this book, Paul is writing to the Corinthians holding the church responsible for disciplining those individuals practicing incest.

In Deuteronomy 22:28–29 rape was strictly forbidden by God. The stories of Dinah and Tamar are examples of how God condemns rape. They show how destruction and devastating pain can be consequences of sexual sin and they also demonstrate how the lives of innocent people can be affected. This seems something to which perpetrators give very little thought.

Dinah was the daughter of Jacob. His family viewed themselves as set apart from others. It was believed God wanted them to remain separate from their neighbors. Dinah was raped by Shechem, the son of Hamor the Hivite. When Jacob and his sons heard about the rape they became distraught and angered. But Hamor out of love for his son went to Jacob and his sons and asked permission for his son to marry Dinah. The marriage was at first denied because the Hivites were not serving the God of Abraham, Isaac, and Jacob. But because Shechem was so enamored with Dinah, his father agreed and all the men of their country agreed to follow God's laws.

Several days later, Dinah's brothers took some men and killed every male in the city. They took their flocks, wealth, women, and their sister and returned home. Now even though they felt justified, many innocent people died and Jacob's sons were cursed as they wrongly pursued what they believed to be justice. This is an example of how devastating the consequences of sexual sin can be.

The story of Tamar is about lust and destruction. In this story, a young man named Amnon convinced himself he was in love with his half sister Tamar. She was very beautiful. Struggling with this issue, he confided in his cousin Jonadab and between the two of them they developed a plan. Amnon was to pretend he was sick and request of his father King David that his sister be allowed come tend to him. But prior to Tamar arriving, Amnon had his servants leave the home so there would be no one to witness his plans as they unfolded. When Tamar arrived her brother coaxed her into his bedroom pretending he could only eat from her hands. When she entered his room, Amnon raped her.

After the rape, Amnon became disgusted with Tamar and had her thrown from his home into the streets. She begged for him not to do that and even asked him to speak to the King so they could be married. Amnon refused and had her disgraced. Because she was no longer a virgin there was no way she could be given in marriage. As a result, she was left to live her life a desolate woman.

When Tamar's brother Absalom heard of his sister's rape, he became outraged. But rather than act immediately, he told his sister this was to remain a family matter. He allowed Tamar to live with him and cared for her. Similar to Absalom, when King David heard about the rape, he did nothing, either. He never confronted Amnon for what is believed to be two reasons. First Amnon was his oldest son and therefore next in line to be king. David also did not punish Amnon because he had been guilty himself of committing adultery with Bathsheba.

As mentioned, Absalom did not act immediately to his anger. He remained patient. Eventually he evolved a plot against Amnon and after two years had him killed.

These stories have elements easily associated with sexual abuse. There is the desire to have selfish physical needs met; there is deceit; efforts to keep the crime a secret or a family matter; there is the eventual destruction of homes and countries; and lastly the taking of innocence, as well as innocent lives.

So often when discussing sexual abuse we only want to talk about children being molested as if that somehow makes it less of a crime. But unfortunately, many children are also raped which makes this even more horrible. A heinous crime with long-standing consequences for the victim and perpetrators, sexual abuse is terribly wrong. It is a sin God has great displeasure for as it is perpetrated against innocent children. God has made it clear that we are to protect the helpless and the innocent. Who more so should we then agree needs help than the children who are victimized in this horrible crime. For surviving adults of sexual abuse, you have a right to be angry and you have a right to heal. You owe it to yourself to stand in agreement with God and fight for your right to freedom.

Chapter 6

RELEASING THE GUARDS

THERE ARE MANY reasons people choose to make certain decisions in their lives. Some of us are motivated by pain, some by opportunities, and some people make decisions because of voids in their lives. My decision to "release the guards" was motivated by the latter. Realizing my life was devoid of peace and love was the impetus for me choosing to finally give my heart a chance to heal. I was in and out of relationships because I had no peace and this habit began to weigh on me. I was developing a great desire to have a healthy long-standing relationship that would lead to marriage.

As I will discuss further in this chapter, "the guards," if you will, were the many issues and emotions I thought I was using to protect myself. These issues included anger, hatred, bitterness, shame, lack of trust, violence, and many others. It took a life filled with ups and downs, in and out of relationships, and other tiring hardships, for me to realize my life had to change. Regardless of my circumstances and no matter what level of intimacy I achieved, I was unable to maintain any significant happiness or satisfaction because I did not have peace. This was completely tied to the fact I had not dealt with the pain of my past. As a result, I became strangely comfortable with the nightmarish, strange world I was placed in. And to some way accept my life as it was,

I eventually developed two negative coping skills: avoidance and denial. While I thought these coping skills would protect me, they continuously caused great confusion and pain in my life.

Through avoidance I attempted to keep myself from circumstances that could remind me of my past. This was done in two ways. First, I avoided interactions with my family, at times going years without seeing them. This was done because I no longer wanted to be close to the people who caused my pain. I also avoided developing high levels of intimacy by moving in and out of different relationships. I wanted to avoid intimacy because I believed if the people who were supposed to be my caregivers would hurt me, so would everyone else.

To complete this task, I developed the debilitating issue of control. I completely controlled things when I saw my family. I controlled relationships through defense mechanisms by always finding fault in others. I also controlled the duration of my intimate relationships by simply moving on when I felt myself becoming too emotionally attached. I was also unfaithful and used the threat of being with someone else as a way to control my relationships.

Due to my need for control, relationships with family and friends remained guarded. It was as if my heart was a palace and I had permanent guards protecting it. Developing new relationships was an entirely threatening proposition and that was generally a slow process. It would take something monumental for me to let someone new close to me. Conversely, something very small could cause me to remove anyone from my life. The sad irony for me and many victims of abuse is the one thing I tried to prevent, which was being hurt again, happened regularly because control issues sabotaged my relationships.

Avoidance eventually led to my denial. Because I thought I was able to avoid any ties to my past, I then believed I could somehow deny the shame, anger, hate, and confusion that were eating away at my heart. If I refused to acknowledge my past pain, these negative emotions could not control me. I was able to "pretend" for brief periods of time, and actually remember going from junior high school to early college rarely remembering my past. This was due in part to the fact that during this time, I had no really significant intimate relationships with females. I dated regularly, but remained emotionally unattached in most of these relationships. This lack of intimacy helped fuel my denial. True intimacy requires honesty, so remaining free of intimacy therefore allowed me to continue wearing a mask and not reveal my true self.

It is interesting to note it took an unpredictable event like pledging a fraternity to cause my childhood issues to resurface. The at times violent nature of the pledging experience returned me to my childhood. It reminded me of the absence of control and the vulnerability I felt when I was being abused. Even though I was able to ignore my past for years, when these emotions resurfaced I had to deal with them. There was the shame that eventually led to self-esteem issues. Anger led to uncontrollable rage and violence, which were clearly related to my developed self-hatred. The hate obstructed my ability and desire to love. And the confusion continuously fueled my inability to trust as well as my overwhelming fear of being hurt. These detrimental issues controlled me throughout most of my adult life. Recognizing this tragedy and the clear absence of peace helped me finally decide to take the necessary steps to healing.

My first step to healing was realizing I had to mentally take my wounded heart across an extremely intimidating bridge and face my past. This would then require me to mentally take my unhealed heart back across that same bridge and begin living a new life. And as I grudgingly learned, *this process would have to be repeated many times.*

This is a critical point because many abused people want to deal with crossing this bridge only once. They want to cross over and dump their issues and baggage, somehow disconnect from their past, and then believe this process will automatically finish healing them. The belief that this can all be done in one fell swoop is regrettably stifling and completely damaging. It leaves many victims living in denial and ultimately prevents them from truly healing.

Many victims of abuse will also cross this bridge one way and then attempt to return across a completely unrelated bridge to healing. For these individuals, the pain from their past becomes a consuming motivation. It drives them to develop certain skills or engage in a variety of activities they believe will improve their damaged self-worth. For example, some victims are driven to pursue and achieve high levels of success in different areas such as sports, education, entertainment, and business to name a few. Others will also pursue opportunities in helping professions allowing them to assist victims of abuse or assist in the prevention of abuse. This becomes very rewarding as it allows victims to shift the focus from their pain to others. These options may help to improve self-esteem and offer some sense of empowerment for these victims by allowing them to mask or temporarily forget about their past. But whether victims become empowered by embracing celebrated lives and activities or by pursuing rewarding opportunities that free them from having to think a lot about their past, it is my contention neither allows them to heal from their past.

Being empowered and healing are two very different issues; coping and healing are two distinct outcomes. The difference is that external empowerments help victims cope better by briefly balancing the weight of negative emotions with positive events or accomplishments. But because this kind of empowerment does not require or assist in removing the weight of negative emotions from the heart, coping (to whatever degree achieved) remains the best result. Healing on the other hand, requires emptying the negative baggage and replacing it with positive emotions. Even though this process may be painful at times, this critical difference allows victims to go beyond coping. It allows them to conquer their past. I know this to be true because I tried using my successes as a way to heal. But no matter what I achieved, I remained emotionally empty. Consequently, my healing was delayed. I now realize remaining connected to, but not imprisoned by your past is essential to the healing process. It is critical for honestly assessing the progression of your healing.

In the twelfth chapter of Matthew, the Bible tells us when a man empties his house of negative forces and sins, it is then extremely important to fill that house with positive forces and the Word and love of God. If the voids left when nega-tive forces are removed are not refilled with positive forces, the likelihood is the old negative forces will eventually return and do even more damage. When victims of abuse begin the healing process and begin ridding themselves of negative baggage, they must be willing to accept, live with, and actively practice behaviors appropriate to the new posi-tive emotions. They in essence have to have their heart and mind reconditioned ultimately preparing themselves for the discomfort of the unfamiliarity of their new health. As the old baggage and guard are released, the task becomes redefining oneself to the extent that you actively begin the practice of doing things differently, saying things differently, and ultimately believing in the process of healing. Just as old habits may die hard, learning new ones can be difficult as well. If this process is not undertaken, the negative emotions will continue to resurface and ultimately cause more damage. I call this the practice of positive replacements. This principle is very practical and it was central to my journey. The actual steps of this process will be discussed later in Chapter 10.

Before discussing my journey, let me first describe the bridge and what it represented. As I mentioned earlier, it took an honest self-examination for me to realize I needed to change. Because of this great need, the bridge would represent a dreaded but vital link to a past I previously refused to face, but now had to confront. It would also represent a vital link to change and an opportunity for a better life. I stood on one side of the bridge and a very difficult past was on the other. Crossing this bridge one way would provide a needed opportunity to confront my issues and pain thereby opening a door to healing. As a result, the trip back across this same bridge would provide hope for my future. These elements were essential to my healing.

While crossing the bridge toward my abusive past, I carried the crippling weight of many negative emotions, including anger, hate, shame, confusion, fear, and an inability to trust and love, to name a few. Crossing over to the other side would provide an opportunity to eventually rid myself of these negative emotions by purposely depositing them on the other side. On the return trip, I would still carry the weight of these negative emotions, but because each trip would allow me to leave portions of theses emotions on that side of the bridge, the weight would not be as heavy returning across the bridge. The burden would also be lessened or offset by the positive emotions I would be able to develop once back on my safe side of the bridge. These emotions included peacefulness, self-esteem, joy, happiness, pride, courage, love of self, and love of others, all of which were essential to my healing. Returning across the bridge with my heart less burdened provided the hope for my new life.

My journey began because I ultimately wanted to learn how to love myself and give love. I also needed to learn how to trust and receive love from others. This process started when I readily owned my hurtful truths. I then boldly faced at that time my worst fear and necessarily confronted the persons who violated me. This was extremely difficult because of the loyalty issues mentioned earlier. It was also difficult because of my great fear of rejection. This is sadly related to the high probability that if confronted, many perpetrators might adamantly refuse to acknowledge any wrongdoing, potentially causing more emotional damage.

A critical point to address at this time is that the initial confrontation, regardless of the outcome, is the springboard to healing. It is my contention that whether the experience is positive or negative, taking this initial step has to be considered a *victory* for victims, even if it may not feel like one at the time. I liken this confrontation to planting a seed of healing. It will be a seed that will ultimately grow, thereby giving victims needed confidence and hope with regard to their ability to sustain a path of growth and separation from the pain of their abuse.

Confronting my perpetrators was my first crossing of the bridge. It allowed me to finally free myself from some of the consuming weight of negative emotions I carried for so many years. I had to let them know I agonizingly remembered what they did to me and how horribly it impacted my life. I had to forgive them, and I had to let go of my anger toward them. This also allowed me to come out from under the blanket of obscurity and be set free emotionally so I could begin taking the required baby steps toward learning to trust and love myself again.

I initially thought I would be able to rid myself of all the negative emotions in one trip. I also believed I would be able receive all the positive emotions when I returned. I was only fooling myself. When I finally made it over the bridge and confronted my perpetrators, it was emotionally draining. The fear I developed over the years from dreading this experience had become overwhelming.

When I crossed the bridge the first time, the only negative emotion I was able to rid myself of was anger. This was made possible through forgiveness, not because my abusers acknowledged their wrongdoing. At the first crossing I began viewing that side of the bridge as the graveyard where I wanted to bury what eventually would become the old me. It was where I buried most of my anger and received some needed peace.

This peace was the only positive emotion I could handle at that time. It was also the only positive emotion I carried back across the bridge along with the remaining weight of negative emotions. It was not complete peace, but nonetheless it was a peace I had not had for many years. It was also the first positive emotion I owned. Receiving it was a prerequisite to developing my ability to continue crossing this bridge.

The first time I crossed the bridge was the only time I dumped a negative emotion and at the same time received a positive one. This was because my need to confront coupled with the anticipation had become so overwhelming. So once I finally crossed that first bridge, completing this monumental task immediately gave me so much needed relief and a certain level of confidence. I was finally able to exhale.

It is important to note here the step to confronting takes absolute resolve. I had to be mentally prepared in case my perpetrators denied the truth. If they did, I would still be required to make peace within myself and forgive them. So while I, in my case, was very fortunate to have them acknowledge their wrongdoings and apologize, it was my own actions that gave me peace. I want to be sure not to give them any credit for anything I did.

Once on my side of the bridge I felt safe and somewhat satisfied with the peace I now had. This state lasted only for a while because for so many years I thought all I needed was to have my perpetrators acknowledge their crime and that would make things OK. But eventually I had to face the fact that this peace was only a bandage. With many issues continuously haunting me, happiness was a distant place and it was difficult seeing my life in a positive light. Consequently and over time, my perceived safe side of the bridge became a challenge as my still wounded heart remained full with emotions that needed to be buried back across the bridge.

Because I continued feeling restless and unfulfilled, my safe side of the bridge eventually came to represent a mirror I would have to face every day. As long as I looked in that mirror and saw a man hurting, I knew I would have to continue making the treks across the bridge for more healing. An important point to be made here is that while my side of the bridge initially represented a mirror that continued to show me how much pain I was in and how much I needed to continue crossing over the bridge, this same mirror also would allow me eventually to see the progress and changes I was making. It would also help me see the new me that was emerging.

My desire for more peace and the fact that other family members had been abused initially led me to continuously cross this bridge and confront my perpetrators. I realized a big part of my healing depended on my ability to confront them and our past. It helped from these confrontations, that I was able to get some answers to the important questions of how and why they could do these things. This allowed me to begin ridding myself of some of my most damaging emotions I felt I had no control of. These were shame, resentment, bitterness, the strange sense of loyalty, and confusion. Again, once on my safe side of the bridge, I was also able to begin learning how to accept and live with the following emotions: self-esteem, a sense of accomplishment; more peace; love of self and others; joy; and happiness for myself and for others.

Each time I made it across the bridge I felt a part of me dying. This would eventually allow a new spirit to grow within my heart and enabled me to begin living as a new person. This process would take several years. Every trip across the bridge allowed me to bury more and more of each negative emotion until they were almost gone or completely gone.

A critical point to this part of the process is the fact that each time I buried a negative emotion across the bridge I would then be left with a void as I returned. It would be on the other side of the bridge, my safe side, where I would then begin to seek ways to fill the void left from burying the negative emotion. It became essential that I actively sought out ways to fill these voids with positive thoughts, feelings and behaviors because if I failed in this process, the voids would more than likely be refilled by even more intense negative emotions.

This back-and-forth process was essential as each trip allowed me to open myself up a little more to family and friends. This in turn made me less guarded as I slowly began to open a door to trusting on an intimate level. Given that I was willing to continue facing myself in the mirror and remained committed to my healing, I was able and willing to continue on my journey. Because of additional trips motivated by social relationships, job experiences, and opportunities to help other victims, I was able to deal with most of my remaining issues and emotions.

It was ultimately a sincere look at failed relationships and my desire to one day have a healthy marriage that forced me to make these treks across the bridge. It is no coincidence the final emotion I buried across the bridge was fear and the final emotions I wanted to learn to live with were trust and love.

Crossing the bridge to bury and gain the previous emotions had been very difficult. Those trips were intimidating because I had to confront my perpetrators. I was able to survive these confrontations because I knew they were helping to heal and develop my heart, and I desperately needed that. But because the man I faced in the mirror had not completely healed, I knew I had to make at least one more trip across the bridge. This trip would not, however, require me to face my perpetrators. Even though our lives would be inextricably tied together, their power had been buried along with my negative emotions. I now had control over my life and emotions. This gave me the ability to complete the most daunting task of my healing.

This final trip would require me to face the person I had slowly buried…"the old me." It would also require me to bury the fear I had previously used to protect myself, alongside that man. This would create an ironic set of circumstances. To complete this final trip, I would have to leave myself without the one emotion that motivated me to protect myself (fear), in order to gain the emotions I was most afraid of, but desperately wanted and needed (trust and love). And that meant I would have to put my newly healed heart in harm's way again. By this I mean if I desired true and uninhibited love, I had to be willing to wholeheartedly trust myself physically and emotionally to someone. Similar to the feelings I had while being abused I would have to become completely vulnerable again.

This is a bridge many abused people refuse to cross. It can be the result of a conscious or unconscious decision and have damaging consequences for existing and future relationships. Burying my fear alongside the "old me" allowed me to finally face and complete this previously impossible task. I was uncomfortably vulnerable, but at peace because of the opportunity I now had to develop love in my heart.

Now this did not mean I was free from past issues, however it did mean my issues would no longer control me. When circumstances arose that caused old memories to resurface, I had to accept my truths and remind myself that I had overcome my pain and past.

I still cross the bridge from time to time because I will always have room for more healing and growth. These bridge crossing experiences may occur when I see my abusers, when I reflect on my own as I often do, through experiences on my job, and they can even take place when I see something on television or in the news. Anything that reminds me of my past causing me to reflect and evaluate my feelings is a bridge crossing experience. It is simply good to be able to cross this bridge because I want to and not so much because I have to.

There are so many victims of physical and emotional abuse who have assumed a life sentence by unnecessarily remaining prisoners to their past. For many, there is a crippling tendency to look externally for assistance to overcome their hurts. This is not to say victims do not need help with the healing process because support systems are very necessary. These may consist of counselors, family members, pastors, support groups, and very close friends, to name a few. But they also need to believe they have a conquering spirit that will enable them to overcome. Victims tend to think they are weak or inadequate because of their suffering. The ironic and great reality is that *they have been made even stronger by enduring what they have been through.* That is what this story is all about. Victims need to realize the courage and inner strength already within them that enables them to face each day can be manifested in a determination and ability to cross their intimidating bridges to healing. They can then allow that same courage and strength to be fully manifested in an unreserved willingness to risk their previously wounded hearts for a love of self and others.

My resolve to be a conqueror was utterly challenged on this journey. Because the trips across the bridge did not always produce desired results, I sometimes had to fight through disappointments and setbacks. I had to remember to not "beat myself up" when I made mistakes and I had to instead "pick myself up" after mistakes and continue on my journey. This required me to be honest with myself and always acknowledge negative feelings when they surfaced.

Prior to this process the norm was to deny the feelings. This point is critical because throughout this entire process, being honest about my feelings was the only way I could truly move forward.

This journey forced me to unmask the man I faced in the mirror and acknowledge the person I was—a victim of abuse. It also allowed me to become the person I am now—a conqueror of abuse. This has been a "walk of faith." My faith in God gave me strength to believe in myself. I believed I could heal and thereby learn to love. No matter where you believe your inner strength comes from, the journey to healing ultimately becomes a matter of making a decision to "release the guards," and commit to the belief that it can be successfully completed, no matter the obstacles.

I realize there are many people who for a variety of reasons have held on to their pain for many years. Some of these people have not confronted their past because the perpetrators have died. I believe this process is viable for them. They can still tell their story, let family and friends support them through this process, and I believe they can spiritually be set free from the pain of their past without the physical presence of the perpetrators. I say this because *healing is about taking power away from the abusers*. If you can confront them, that is even better. But if you are unable to confront them because they are dead, I believe this process can still take place in your heart.

Chapter 7

THE GOD OF COMFORT

I HAVE OFTEN WONDERED about my life and questioned why I was abused. I now understand my journey. The Word of God reads in 2 Corinthians 1:3–4, "Praise be to the God…of compassion and…of all comfort, who comforts us in all our troubles, so that we can comfort those in any trouble with the comfort we ourselves have received from God." This scripture has become one of the cornerstones of my faith, as it clearly speaks to my heart.

Throughout my journey, there were many times when I adopted a very selfish attitude about my life. As was detailed through my pity parties and all the many negative emotions I lived with coupled with the negative behaviors I was involved in, it was very apparent I was not interested in anyone else's wants, thoughts, or needs. My life was all about me and at times the few close friends I allowed in my "inner circle." And then life became just about us few. I am reminded of a quote from a dear friend who was also abused. She used to say that she only had herself and three friends. Her motto was, "Us four and no more!" While my world never became that small, the essence of her life's theme was lived by me and I am sure by many abused children and adults.

I can remember continuously telling myself throughout my pity parties, I was one of the most victimized if not the most victimized person to ever walk this earth. It is kind of interesting to note here, while I did not ask for help or readily extend myself or concern myself with other people's problems, I have always had an ability to be very nurturing and comforting to those in pain. I became a reliable friend and confidant to many of my peers and many of them have told me how much they depended on me.

I can remember disappearing for a while and not communicating with any of my friends as I was going through some personal issues. When I resurfaced and confided in one of my friends he immediately became mad and said to me, "You do not have the right to disappear and take care of personal matters because too many people need and depend on you. You are supposed to be our rock!" I appreciated the fact that I was needed so much, but this set of circumstances epitomized my life in an ironic way. I did not actively show my feelings or how much I cared about people, however I had a need to be depended on and enjoyed the moments when I was. I guess these moments allowed me to feel some sense of normalcy, as they were the rare moments when I could show and feel my own sensitive side. I needed to know that side of me existed.

Along with my selfish attitude, I also developed a hard personality. While I would always try to be sensitive to others, it was often difficult for me to be sensitive to my own feelings and needs. Consequently I often became a martyr. Things had to become really bad for me before I would tell anyone and even then I only told people when I knew they could not impact my circumstances. In some sick way this allowed me to continue not to trust or rely on others, even in circumstances that were my own fault. I never gave friends or family a real opportunity to help me during my times of need. I wanted to be that "rock," as my friend called me, and

I did not want to have to depend on anyone. At times, that also included God. I remember a good friend of mine asking me if I remembered the last time I cried. I told her I did not, but I knew it was many, many years earlier. I had become so hard and devoid of so many emotions that I was not even able to cry at my own father's funeral.

I have since come to realize in so many ways how much God kept me even though my personality evolved the way it did. When I was thinking no one cared about me and it appeared as such, God was always there, keeping me out of harm's way and carrying me through a lifetime of pain and disappointments. I always thought I was alone. I can see now my thoughts were as far from the truth as the "east is from the west." With this new knowledge, I have also been made to see and understand my life's journey.

While I wish I had not been abused, I understand were it not for my abuse, I would not have become the man I am today. Just as I was allowed to go deep into the lowest pits of despair and experience the tragic lows from my many negative emotions and behaviors, God has taken me on the other end of the spectrum and allowed me to experience the extreme highs on the other end. With hate and anger gone from my heart, I now love deeply and hard. My heart is open. My true self can be seen—my true self is a man who desires to help others. This is the essence of this chapter.

I understand my journey was one I had to take. It has led me to become the man I am. A man who desires to assist and comfort others in pain and more specifically, someone who desires to comfort those individuals who have also been victims of abuse. Had I not gone through what I did as a child, I would have never been able to have the deep level of compassion and love I have for children and people who are hurting. Had I not had my life experiences, I could not feel led by God to write this story with hopes that it will offer hope and inspiration to other victims of abuse to set out on their own journey to healing. God comforted me throughout my life and I now understand I have to render that same comfort and support to as many people as I can reach.

My story is an attempt to help others heal. I am a Clinical Social Worker and I have worked with many abused children and adults. It is my desire through this book to get people to talk more about this horrible crime, to show it is more prevalent than people want to admit, and to offer hope and inspiration to other sexually abused children and adults. I hope this book will get enough people talking about this crime such that it can prevent the abuse of any more innocent children.

The Word of God reads in Ephesians 6:12 (KJV), "For we wrestle not against flesh and blood, but against principalities, against powers…against spiritual wickedness in high places." This story is about revealing a lie the enemy has kept secret for many years. It is about helping free the many people who have been wrongly imprisoned physically, mentally, and emotionally as a result of sexual abuse. The enemy does not want them to know about healing for he "roams about seeking whom he may destroy" (1 Pet. 5:8, author's paraphrase). My abuse is but one of the many "crosses" I may have to bear as a Christian. My story is a testimony to God and a story I was destined to tell.

Chapter 8

INTENDED HARM
TURNED GOOD

OR MANY YEARS prior to confronting my abusers, I made a conscious decision to stay away from home. This was the only way I could cope with my past and for me it was the safest way. I was living a life filled with so much rage and violence. I knew going home would possibly put me in the paths of the men who violated me and I also knew seeing either one of them would easily present the potential for harm either to them or to me. You see I spent a lot of my time thinking about harming them and I even considered killing them. More than five years passed without my going home for any holidays or even to visit. I would call and that was the extent of my involvement with any of my family members. But having made contact by now and having successfully confronted both men and having them acknowledge their crime, going home now became something I had to do.

Several years after I confronted the men who molested me I went home to visit during the summer. While I was home I decided to confide in one of my older sisters and tell her about my experience. As I began to share my story she immediately began to cry and comfort me. Thinking it was simply that, I told her I was involved in counseling and I was determined through God's help to enjoy my complete healing.

She expressed great joy at my determination and resolve, but then slowly pulled away from me. I was not quite sure why she pulled away and because she continued to listen I did not question her actions. Much to my surprise however, she then began to ask me very specific questions as to time, circumstances surrounding my abuse, specific details, and much more. Even though I was caught off guard by the swiftness with which she inundated me with questions, I immediately felt safe and comforted as I told myself telling her was the right thing to do.

After several hours of talking and sharing, my sister leaned over on her chair and began to cry heavily. For some reason I began to feel the need to comfort her. I told her she did not need to feel that sorry for me because I was going to be OK. She then grabbed my hands and told me there was something she wanted to tell me. She first started by saying, "My tears are not only for you." I remember looking at her in a strange way and then quickly asked her, "What do you mean?" She then began to squeeze my hands and told me that one of my abusers had violated her, also.

To this day, I still do not have the words to describe the emotions I felt at that moment. Just as I was beginning to enjoy the comfort of knowing that someone in my family now shared my secret and most importantly still accepted me, I immediately began to feel the rage I had felt for so many years. But this time it was for a different reason. I have four sisters. I have always had a great deal of respect and love for each and every one of them. And for me to now hear that this precious jewel, my dear sister, had experienced the same thing I did, sent me spiraling backward. The more we talked the more I felt that uncontrollable rage from my past and I began entertaining serious thoughts of doing great harm to this man. But praise God, He comforted us and gave us peace as we looked to each other for answers and a way to bring our truths out.

We continued to talk throughout the day and evening, trying somehow to comfort each other while swimming in a consuming disbelief that these horrible things had actually happened in the confines of our home without anyone knowing a thing. Rather quickly we came to the conclusion that it must have happened to others, too. We wrestled with exploring it with our other siblings. Even though we were filled with a tremendous amount of emotion and energy, we eventually resolved ourselves to trying to manage our secrets for now and decided before we dug any deeper we would try to help each other out as much as possible. As we continued to talk I shared with my sister how I confronted the men who abused me. She was quite taken by the fact that both men readily admitted their wrongdoing and apologized. She mentioned to me that one main reason she kept her secret for so long was because of her fear of rejection and the damage it might do to the family. I told her I completely understood those emotions as it took me many years to get the courage to confront my abusers.

I stayed home that summer for about a week. My sister and I continued to talk about our experiences and one of the things she desired was for me to help her confront her abuser as well. We decided I would and it was determined that I would go to her abuser for her and let him know I knew and she also remembered what he did to her. Our hope of course was that after our conversation, he would go to my sister, allow her to express her feelings and emotions, and ultimately acknowledge his crime and offer a truly heartfelt apology. As I knew with my circumstances, my sister understood that her feelings needed to be validated and she also knew she was going to have to forgive this man for what he did. Her hope was that she could tell him she forgave him after they talked. I left home on that weekend with the plan of contacting our abuser and talking with him about my sister.

As I promised my sister, I made contact with our abuser and made arrangements for us to talk. I informed him I knew about my sister and we needed to talk. My hope was he would bypass me and go straight to my sister, but he preferred to talk with me first. Much to my surprise he agreed and we made arrangements to meet at home during the holiday. I knew my sister would not be home during this time and I felt like this had the potential for working out.

For as long as I can remember, I do not believe I have ever experienced anything or any emotions like I experienced the night I met with our abuser. We met at my mother's house and decided to take a ride around the corner so we could talk at the park. I remember being filled with so much anger and fear. I had no idea how this was going to turn out and quite honestly, I wished I had not agreed to take on this task. Nonetheless, we made it to the park and began to talk. I shared my sister's story with our abuser and he surprisingly acknowledged his wrongdoing. I impressed upon him the need to go to my sister and talk with her. While I knew he was listening, in my heart I did not feel as though he would.

Now this man is one of the hardest and meanest persons I have ever known in my life. When we talked about the things he did to me, he did cry, but his emotions were nothing like what he expressed as we talked about my sister. He began to shake and almost immediately began to cry and apologize. All he could say was, "I'm going to hell. God will not forgive me for the things I've done. I'm not worthy!" As he was expressing his emotions and regret, a part of me began to feel some vindication and I even thought to myself, "Yeah, you should be sorry," and "You're no good for doing these things to us!" I went so far to say to him, "Yes, you were wrong," and asked him how he could do such horrible things to children. At that moment I know my intent was to make him feel as bad as I could. But as my rage began to surface, I was convicted in my heart. I became challenged spiritually to comfort this man and if that was not enough, a burning desire filled my heart to talk with him about God's love and the gift of salvation through Jesus Christ.

I resisted these thoughts for a while and told myself surely these feelings must be a joke. How dare God ask or even expect me to show this kind of love to a man I had determined was not deserving of it. So I did continue to prod him as I was determined to dole out some measure of revenge. But before I could go too far, I was convicted again. The Lord let me know that I was in no position to judge. As the Lord reminded Job, I, too, was reminded that I, "was not there when He laid the earth's foundation, I cannot give orders to the morning…and I have no command over the winds or the stars" (Job 38, author's paraphrases).

I was therein politely reminded that moments like these were designed in heaven so we can see God's hands at work. I apologized to God in my heart and with the feelings in my heart and His Spirit consuming me, I was led that evening to share with this man about God's grace and forgiveness and how he could still have a relationship with God. I told him God would forgive him for his sins and all he had to do was repent. I also told him God would not only heal my sister and me, but that God would heal him, too. With tears continuing to race from his eyes, he said, "You believe God will forgive me for what I've done?" I told him yes and he did ask God to forgive him. I do not know what decisions he made that night, but he did tell me he was going to talk with God on his own. He said if I could tell him about God's love under our circumstances there must be something to it.

It is important to note here how God challenges our resolve. I have spoken throughout this book how we must use our resolve to fight the good fight, to become overcomers. Well this is an example of how God challenged my resolve in a manner that required me to humble myself and my will to His. I had to accept humility and swallow my pride as to what I thought was right and what I wanted in order to obey God and share His love with this man.

I am not sure if this man accepted Christ later that night, but he was in church the next morning with my family. Never in my wildest dreams did I ever think I would be led to witness to and share God's abounding and unfailing love and grace with a man who raped and violated me for more than a year. This is the God I serve, and I thank Him that I was able to obey His will.

This is truly an example of how God takes what the enemy intends for bad and turns it into good. Just as God protected Joseph from the attacks of the enemy so His will could be done in Egypt, He also protected me throughout my life so I could be used to show His forgiveness and share His love with my abusers. Even though I was abused and had for a great part of my life lived with pain and self-destructive behavior, the Lord saw fit to bring me out of my life of despair, by saving my soul and healing my heart. He then made ultimate use of what the enemy intended for bad, by then allowing me to share His love and the gift of salvation with the very man the enemy used to cause my pain.

Chapter 9

THE RECOVERING VICTIM
OF SEXUAL ABUSE

*A*s I MENTIONED in the previous chapter, I have lived a very challenging life. All of my ups and downs have over the course of time made me a much stronger man. My resolve has been strengthened with regard to who I am to myself. I am no longer weighed down with the need or desire to measure up to anyone else's standards. I now have to answer to God and my desire is for Him to control my footsteps. But these facts notwithstanding, I am still reminded of my abuse and I stay mindful of where I came from and the journey to get where I am.

It would be so easy for me to take for granted the blessing of deliverance from the Lord. I know the enemy would have me to think everything is OK now and I can move forward on my own. That would be the worst decision I could ever make in my life. I got where I am today with the help of the Lord. I realize that in order for me to continue to grow and prosper, in order for me to continue healing and even more importantly in order for me to do God's will and somehow allow Him to use my life as a testimony of His grace and mercy, I will have to stay connected with God even more now and never allow myself to believe I can continue on this journey by myself. I have to maintain this attitude no matter how good I feel and no matter what the enemy tries to tell me.

The Word of God tells us the "word is a lamp to my feet and a light for my path" (Ps. 119:105). It took me a long time to understand this scripture. Now that I do, it has real meaning to me.

When I began my journey to healing, all I could see was the big picture. Looking back on my life, I can see now where that particular mind-set was in and of itself one of my biggest roadblocks. Because I would only look at the big picture, it was easy for the enemy to distract me from where I knew in my heart I wanted and needed to be. You see, the big picture looked so intimidating. I could see all the bumps in the roads ahead of me, all the pending trials and tribulations and most importantly when looking at the big picture the only person I saw on the journey was me. I realize now God was there all the time, but when I was looking at things through my own eyes, it appeared that this journey was one I should not take. I had already lived a life where the people who were the closest to me had repeatedly caused me the most significant pain in my life. This again made the journey appear even more daunting as I made up in my mind early on that I did not have anyone I could trust to help and support me consistently. I often looked for people to trust, but eventually told myself not to trust anyone for a long time. That is what I did for the majority of my life.

Looking at the big picture made me believe I could not and would not make the journey. It was easy for me to allow my fears of more pain and disappointment to take control. And when they did, they exacted a heavy measure of doubt in my mind. It was too much of a task for me. Even though I was not happy where I was, I was comfortable. My pity parties were comfortable and they allowed me to stay in a place that was familiar to me. I did not dare want to risk something familiar, albeit my familiar places were horrible places, for an unknown with no guarantees.

Sometimes our lives will be filled with uncertainties and the only thing we can do is take life one second, one minute, one hour, and one day at a time. Survival on this level is something I believe many people struggle with. I certainly did. The point I want to make here is that when one begins the journey to healing from sexual abuse, it will require a lot of baby steps.

When I consider this journey from start to finish, I am amazed at how the most significant gains occurred when I was patient and not expecting too much from myself, too much from my friends, and too much from God. I also experienced more success and healing when I did not try to do too much myself. We can often be our own worst enemies when we are not patient and when we do not wait on the Lord.

This journey had to be a process. I had to make myself accept this fact. After I allowed myself to accept this truth I began to develop the patience required for healing from sexual abuse or any kind of abuse for that matter. I also had to constantly remind myself if I was going to have a relationship with the Lord, this process was going to have to be directed by Him. He was going to have to captain my ship. It was not my place to try and force things, to do things the way I thought they should be done, to decide on what was necessary and what was not, and I certainly could not turn and run every time I was faced with the hard decisions. My faith in God has been tested throughout this journey. I know that God has not let me down. I know now without a doubt that when things went wrong, it was generally because I took some matters into my own hand.

This road obviously has not always been easy. As a matter of fact, I cannot say it has been easy at all. This is why I consider myself a recovering victim of sexual abuse. I believe I have been healed from the pain of my sexual abuse. But my daily reality is that with every day that passes, I can receive a little more strength and peace and consequently my healing becomes even greater. To this end I have often likened myself to a recovering alcoholic, but only to the extent that I realize I have to stay prayerful every day.

There are also several things I have become accustomed to doing that are required to help me keep peace and give me strength. I have to seek and obey God's will for me on a daily basis. I have to strengthen my resolve through the Word of God and I have to think, think, think before I act. While the Lord has truly delivered me from violence, hatred, and my rage, I still take it upon myself to surround myself with people I know understand me and people I know will do everything to protect me now. My trust level has increased as a result of my relationship with God and He has put people in my life to assist me with my daily struggles.

I will never forget what happened to me as a child. I do not want to. When I am reminded of it, I simply choose to praise God as I am thankful that He saw fit to heal me. I could have very easily ended up dead by now or in prison. Had it not been for the Lord rescuing me, something devastating, something terribly bad was destined to happen to me. For this reason, likened to the recovering alcoholic, I will never take any measure of my healing for granted. I will never take the journey itself for granted. I am reminded daily of the many pitfalls of my life. I am reminded of the great amount of self-destruction I engaged in. And I am reminded daily of the great harm I have done to others. Because I have no desire to return to that person and because I desire to continue to grow and strengthen my relationship with the Lord, I will continue to view myself as a recovering victim of sexual abuse. This way I will remain humble as I continue to remind myself that all of my thoughts and actions will have a direct impact on my continued journey to an even greater healing.

Chapter 10

THE PRACTICE OF POSITIVE REPLACEMENTS

T HIS STORY HAS been about making choices and taking the incredibly difficult journey to healing. It has been about taking on unbelievable challenges and having my resolve tested to the limit. Looking back on my mistakes, and because making this journey was such an enormous task, I now understand there are four essential elements (prerequisites, if you will) that should be in place before beginning such a journey. I did not have all of these elements in place before beginning my journey. Some were in place and some I learned along the way.

The first prerequisite is to have a foundation or some kind of strength to rely on while on this journey. I had this element in place. My foundation is prayer and the Word of God. During my difficult times, I relied on God, prayer, a number of scriptures, and stories from the Bible from which to draw strength and inspiration. Whether you are a Christian or not, it is necessary to have something or someone as a go-to source of strength when times get rough. And believe me, they will.

The second prerequisite is a fundamental belief in oneself. I learned this along the way. I discussed in Chapter 6 that it is common for victims of sexual abuse to see themselves as weak and inadequate. This could not be any further from the truth. Second Corinthians 12:10 reads, "For when I am weak, then I am strong." Through our weaknesses God makes us stronger. The simple fact that you endured the sexual abuse and faced each day, regardless of your condition, showed an unparalleled resolve and inner strength. Even though you may bend a lot and surely feel like giving up, facing each day shows you have not given up the fight. As you continue on this journey, your strength and resolve will be tested and grow. If you choose to believe in yourself, and choose to believe you can heal, it can and will happen. It will be a process, but it will happen.

The third prerequisite is an unwavering commitment to the process. I also had this element in place. My life was in such disarray that I knew I had to stay committed once I began this process. Giving up could not be an option. As was also discussed in Chapter 6, the need to continue pushing forward is very important. You will have setbacks throughout this journey and may become weakened as a result. How you handle those setbacks will determine how far you will go in your healing. You must remember to not beat yourself up when things go wrong. You must instead pick yourself up, learn from your mistakes, and continue moving forward regardless of your feelings and circumstances. Remember if you fail to continue moving forward, you then leave a door open for the negative emotions to return. Also remember Philippians 4:13, "I can do everything through him who gives me strength."

The final prerequisite that should be in place before beginning this journey is complete honesty. I also had to learn this along the way. You must face each day assessing yourself and be willing to always acknowledge your true feelings whether good or bad. When I did this, I would always pray and ask

God to "meet me where I am, at my point of need." Only then could I begin each day facing what was truly in my heart thereby truly addressing my issues.

With this honesty, you must also have an understanding that you cannot rely on your emotions to get through this journey. If you approach this journey relying on your emotions, you will eventually be defeated. I say this because as we know, our emotions can be all over the place. They can be tossed by your moods and leave you feeling like you are riding on a roller coaster. I am not saying to not enjoy the good feelings. But I am saying if we are not careful, our emotions can easily give us a false sense of security. And when that blanket is taken away you can be caught off guard by a wealth of negative emotions that can send you spiraling backward.

As I previously discussed, the confrontations with my abusers were only the beginning of my healing. Owning our truths and going to them helped to release some of my anger. I readily expressed my feelings towards them and the pain I lived with for so many years. It was to say the least, a very emotional event. I was very fortunate they apologized and thank God, I forgave them, because not until that moment did I begin to feel a small part of me healing.

You may or may not confront your abusers. I believe it is the best thing to do. You may not be able to because they are dead. Regardless of your circumstances, if you choose not to confront, you still have to own your truths. You can write letters and maintain journals to express your feelings and emotions and keep them for yourself. I believe this will still be helpful as it can be the beginning of your healing.

Having our truths out in the open gave me some much-needed peace. Because I was blanketed for so many years by the fear of rejection, the fortunate outcomes from these initial confrontations allowed me to finally "breathe." The weight from living a lie for so long was finally off my back. But let me reiterate it was not my abusers who gave me peace. It was my own actions and forgiveness that gave me peace. This is a very important point because whether you are able to confront your abuser(s) or not and whether or not they admit their wrong and apologize, you are still responsible for how you handle that and the rest of your healing. Again the abusers do not have any power over you. That is a lie we victims tend to accept and live with our entire lives. The real power of healing is within you and that power must be accompanied with forgiveness.

My first step with regard to "practicing positive replacements" or cleaning my heart was to address my "bulls in the china store." By this I mean I had to immediately address the very obvious issues that were clearly destroying my life. I had two "bulls" if you will. They were alcohol and marijuana. I knew I had to stop drinking and smoking. If I were to get anywhere on my journey, these habits had to go. And not only did they have to go, I had to replace them with positive activities.

These issues did not go away immediately. I was able to stop using marijuana fairly quickly as I simply chose to stay away from friends who smoked. But stopping the drinking was a process.

Because I drank so heavily, especially on weekends, I had to really seek out friends and activities where it was less likely I would drink. These were few and far between as most of my closest friends drank. My only option as I saw it at the time was to spend time with the few friends who did not drink a lot. I also made myself get involved in activities on the weekends where alcohol would not be present. I would go to church, to the movies, and sometimes I would just stay at home and watch television or read my Bible. The more I became involved in these other activities, the less I drank. Looking back now, I probably should have also joined an Alcoholics Anonymous group.

It took a long time to get out of this habit. It was indeed a process. I cannot say I completely stopped drinking during this journey. There were periods of times when I did not drink at all (I believe the longest period was close to two years). But for the most part what I did do was change what I drank and the frequency. I stopped drinking liquor completely for a long period of time. I would occasionally drink beer, but eventually came to the point where if I was going to drink it would be wine. And that would typically be with dinner. I still drink occasionally today, but nowhere near the extent I did in my past. About two years after I began this process, I was able to see how much my life was beginning to change. I was nowhere near as aggressive or violent, and my health improved.

Getting rid of these destructive habits was essential for my success. Because so many of my negative behaviors were intensified by my drinking and smoking, it was clearly obvious they had to go immediately.

You have to decide what your "bulls in the china store" are. Yours may be excessive eating habits, perverse sexual activities, or many other compulsive behaviors. Once you identify them, the task of removing them will be difficult. But once you begin to see how much they are tied to your negative issues and how much your life will begin to change as these "bulls" disappear, the struggle to shed them will eventually become easier because you will begin to see the benefits. Just remember to take baby steps and do not try to do everything at one time.

I recently completed what would prove to be one of my most rewarding experiences in counseling. I participated in a twelve-week support group with men who had either been sexually abused or who were the abusers. Needless to say this experience was very intense and yet inspiring at the same time. I say this because it allowed me to see other men who either had or were still dealing with the rage I once had. It also provided an opportunity to learn more strategies for dealing with anger.

As I mentioned in my discussion of "releasing the guards" anger was my most prominent issues/guard. I was able to keep people at bay through my anger, violence, and rage. By doing so I believed in my mind I was protecting myself. No one wanted to be around me when I hit my boiling point. Even though I thought I would feel some satisfaction from being left alone, pushing people away through my violence served only one purpose. It made me lonelier.

Dealing with my anger was a tremendous task. Clearly removing the drinking and smoking helped significantly. But because the pain from my past was so intense, getting rid of "the bulls" was only the beginning.

My first line of defense or strategy as I began battling my anger was prayer. I went to God and asked Him to remove the "stones in my heart" that were preventing me from having a better relationship with Him. The Word of God tells us when we pray we are to believe our prayer has been answered. According to Romans 4:17, we are to call things "that are not as though they were." Even though I was just beginning my journey, I had to claim my healing through God before it actually happened. While on this journey I began every day asking God to protect me from the enemy and from myself. And I believe He did. I would also pray endlessly throughout the day for God's assistance and for patience. Prayer is essential. It was used while dealing with all of my negative issues and it was very instrumental in my learning to accept and live with positive emotions.

I learned a great deal from my many counseling sessions. I learned several tips to use when I would get upset. One of the most important ones was simply learning to count to ten before I reacted to people or circumstances that made me angry. It was amazing how such a simple act would help me. Since I was such a reactive person, never thinking first, this tip gave me an opportunity to at least think even if it was briefly, about my feelings, and what my actions might be. It would also provide me or the other person a small window of opportunity to leave the situation completely before anything bad happened. Now do not get me wrong, I frequently had to count to ten many, many, *many* times when I initially began this process and this was all about my learning patience. And this certainly took time.

Another strategy I learned through my counseling was that it would be extremely important for me to stay away from those people and situations I knew had clear potential for causing me anger. Conversely, I had to learn to interact with people who made me comfortable and who were not threatening. This meant I had to stop going to parties like I did. There were certain people in my life I had to stay away from, at least initially. Some of them were close friends and family members. I also had to stay away from situations where I knew I would be tempted to drink. I had to take baby steps during this process because making these changes often meant I might have to be by myself, which would again leave me lonely.

Beginning a serious exercise routine became another strategy I adopted to help deal with my anger and rage. I took this to an extreme for many years and as a result I recently had hernia surgery. Nonetheless, exercising can be a great release of negative energy if done properly. It would be more difficult for me to get as intensely angry and show my rage after I spent so much time in the gym.

Rethinking the way I would interact with people when I got mad also became a strategy for me. I literally chose to process and often practiced with someone what I would say or do when certain circumstances occurred. I had to learn to make myself say to people "It's OK," "Don't worry about it," or "I forgive you," when I became angry. I would also quote Scripture when I felt myself getting angry. I would reflect back on stories from the Bible where people showed kindness and forgiveness during times when they could have been unforgiving and shown hatred. I would sing comforting songs as well as praise God for my victory especially during the times when I felt the most defeated. I ultimately got to the point where I allowed myself to learn how to be another person. I accepted the fact that I needed to develop a new heart.

Lastly, I continued to pursue counseling. To this day, I regularly participate in counseling if for no other reason but to re-evaluate my progress. I cannot overstate the value of individual and group counseling. Support groups are also very beneficial. I spent many months working on my anger before I attempted to address my next "guard" because again, it had been such a dominating force in my life.

Before discussing my next "guard" it is important to

remember the process. I would over time, eventually be working on different issues at the same time. This in and of itself, made this process what it was...a journey. Having said this, the next issue I chose to address was my hatred.

The Word of God tells us we are to "love your neighbor as yourself" (Rom. 13:9). I could not love nor live any of the experiences associated with love because I hated myself so much. As a result, my hatred was categorically tied to my anger.

My heart was filled with extreme hate as I spent so much of my life living with anger. Because of the shame from my abuse, I knew I had a great amount of hatred toward myself, my circumstances, and at times I hated my family and some of my closest friends. My hatred ran so deep I could not stand to see other people happy or successful, and I can remember going in to a rage just from seeing someone smile. The only people I enjoyed seeing happy were children.

I hated feeling as though I was the only one hurting. As a result, when I became enraged I often wanted other people to hurt simply because I wanted the satisfaction of knowing someone else felt the same depth of pain I was feeling. It did not matter if their pain came by my hands. I was filled with so much hatred. I just wanted and needed to see someone, anyone beside myself, in pain. This was a sad state of affairs as I clearly drew a great deal of satisfaction from this behavior.

As was the case when addressing my anger, my first line of defense against hatred was the Word of God. In it I was able to find instruction, comfort, and hope with regard to overcoming my hatred. I knew it was important to get rid of this hatred because it was causing me to sin.

While in prison, Paul wrote to the Philippians instructing them to "rejoice in the Lord always...do not be anxious about anything, but in everything, by prayer and petition with thanksgiving, present your requests to God…and the God of understanding…will guard your hearts and your minds" (Phil. 4:4–7). This story has always amazed me. How could a man in prison find a way or reason to rejoice? This became an example for me live by as Paul demonstrated how he could find joy in the midst of his circumstances regardless of what they are. He was able to do so because of his relationship with the Lord. While I was not in a physical prison, my life was spent in an emotional one. So I chose to believe just like Paul, with God's help, I too could find joy in the midst of my circumstances. This gave me hope and something to believe in. Maintaining this hope became one of my strategies to dealing with my hatred.

I stated in the beginning of this chapter I believe honesty needs to be in place in order to make this journey. This was again, however, one of the things I had to learn along the way because being honest with myself would eventually become an effective strategy to dealing with my hatred. As I began to address at my hatred I had to look for its origin. When I was dealing with my anger, it was easy to justify my behavior because I could readily point to specific things people said or did to make me angry. When dealing with my hatred, I was not able to do that. That was because when I took an honest assessment at why I hated the people I did, the bottom line was they did nothing to make me hate them. My own issues were driving me to hate them. Consequently, I had to look deeper at my hatred and for its origin.

After extended periods of denial and continuing to blame others for my hatred, I was forced to finally accept a truth I was afraid to admit. My hatred was directed at God. I hated Him for allowing me to be abused and I did not know how to deal with this. My heart and mind would ask "How dare you be angry with or hate God?" To which I would respond that I really wasn't, always deferring it back to family and friends. But the more I looked within my heart, the more it became so clear my anger and hatred towards God were very real issues. This left me faced with my ultimate decision. What was I going to do about my relationship with the Lord?

I mentioned earlier in the book my relationship with the Lord was frequently on and off. These feelings were the primary reasons why. I was afraid of God and I was afraid to go to Him and say how I really felt. I knew I wanted a relationship with the Lord, but I was not sure how to go about developing one, especially with so much anger and bitterness in my heart toward Him. Most importantly, I did not want to risk making God mad at me.

It took many, many years for me to develop my relationship with the Lord. The key to my success which I am submitting as another strategy for dealing with my hatred was being completely honest with God. The more honest I was, without what I thought would be reprisals, the more comfortable I became in our relationship. Consequently, and over time, by studying the Word of God, attending church regularly, fellowshiping with friends, and most importantly having very frequent talks with God, my relationship with Him began to feel somewhat intimate and I began to feel as though He did care for me. And even though the haunting question of "why" remained in my mind, I was developing a confidence that question would be answered.

It is no coincidence the more my relationship with God developed the more my anger and hatred towards Him was assuaged. As a result, it was no surprise that over time, my feelings toward my family and friends began to change. I began to see how I mistreated them and I wanted so much to make amends. I still harbored negative emotions towards my abusers along the way, but God's peace in my heart became a weapon against the hatred. I enjoyed the peace tremendously. I also enjoyed not being bogged down with the exacting weight from my anger and hatred.

Another strategy I employed while dealing with my hatred was forgiveness. I had to first ask God to forgive me. I wrongly judged Him and wrongly blamed Him for my circumstances. As I stated in Chapter 7, "The God of Comfort," I eventually learned God had a plan for my life, which in no small way included telling my story.

Secondly, I had to reach out to as many of the people I mistreated along the way as I could, and ask for their forgiveness. I had to accept humility and admit my wrongdoings, which meant I had to ask them to forgive me for the bitterness and jealousy they paid for because of my abuse. I then had to begin treating my family, friends, and even people I did not know, the way I wanted to be treated.

Lastly, I had to forgive myself. I incurred an incredible amount of guilt from my actions, which generally led to me beating myself up. My defense against this behavior became learning to forgive myself. This was something I would not have done in the past as I would have typically spiraled downwardly when I hurt people. Now most people probably did not think I had a conscience, but I always have. I spent many nights crying over my behavior, filled with deep regret. Humbling myself, asking for forgiveness, and forgiving myself added so much more peace to my heart, which in turn contributed to my hatred disappearing.

Lastly, as was the case with my anger, continuing to stay

involved in counseling and support groups proved to be an effective strategy when dealing with my hatred.

Anger and hatred were the "meat and potatoes" on my journey. Because they were such taxing burdens on my heart, I had to often fight through disappointments and setbacks. I was so consumed by them they also fueled and reinforced my other "guards" which made this journey become what it was. Nonetheless I remained true to my cause and continued believing I could heal. I was able to continue believing because I began to see how removing anger and hatred from my heart was already beginning to impact my other issues in a positive way.

The Word of God continued as the first line of defense while addressing my bitterness and jealousy. But this time it proved to be for another reason. Romans 12:15 states we are to "rejoice with those who rejoice; mourn with those who mourn." In the Book of Obadiah we are told "to not look down on your brother in the day of his misfortune nor rejoice...in the day of their destruction" (Obad. 1:12). These scriptures became my reference points. They consistently resonated throughout my heart as they specifically contradicted the way I lived. They were and to some degree, still are challenging. I mentioned earlier how much I hated seeing other people happy. It was easier for me to mourn with someone than it was to celebrate someone else's success.

Learning to be more sympathetic and rejoice with others was a monumental task. I felt like no one supported me through my good or bad times so why should I? Living a life filled with so much pain made it even more difficult.

As my relationship with God continued to grow I began to notice my attitude changing. By this I mean my motivations for dealing with my issues began to change. For example, I viewed dealing with my anger and hatred as being all about me. When it came time to deal with some of my other issues it became about my relationship with God. As I mentioned in the previous scriptures God is very specific with regard to His expectations of us. We are to be there for others when needed and celebrate others' successes.

The point I am trying to make here is that my attitude began to change because I was developing a desire to obey and please God. Because of my relationship with Him I began to see a lot of my actions as sins and I wanted to stop sinning as much as I could. Now do not get me wrong. I am not trying to say that I became a perfect man. I was still tempted with many sinful thoughts and I often fell. But my attitude about my behavior became different.

I also began to see something that surprised and challenged me to my core. I began to realize in order for me to truly heal, my life was going to have to be just as much, if not more at times, about other people. The more I gave of myself to others the more I would heal. And this would become my irony amongst ironies. As much as I felt my innocence, my existence, and true identity were taken away from me with my abuse…as much as I lived every day feeling as though I had no more to give, my reality had slowly become that in order for me to heal, I was going to have dig deeper and give even more of myself to others than I thought I had lost. In other words, my healing was going to require me to someway become unselfish.

As I began dealing with my bitterness and jealousy, I knew my focus had to change. I could not allow myself to go into my "pity parties" when I had these feelings and I had to continue practicing the same principles I used when dealing with my anger. I had to acknowledge my feelings, admit they were wrong, pray and ask God to strengthen me, and then ultimately I had to make a decision. Either I was going to continue to pout and act immature or I was going to try and be an adult and put forth an honest effort to stop being so jealous and bitter. I chose to stop being so jealous and bitter.

I made myself interact more with the people I was jealous of and even told them about my feelings towards them. I would do the same with regard to those people I showed bitterness towards. And as I mentioned when dealing with my hatred, I tried to apologize to those people I mistreated and offended with my behavior. I also continued my practice of learning to forgive myself when I was not successful at fighting my bitterness and jealousy. Lastly as I would do when dealing with my anger, I literally had to practice or role play in counseling sessions, situations where I could use words such as "congratulations," "I'm happy for you," and "I'm sorry," to name a few.

I learned my final strategy for fighting my bitterness and jealousy from a dear friend. This was a life lesson I will cherish forever. When I decided to confront my abusers, the letters were sent in January of that year. We did talk on the phone a couple of times, but I was not able to see them until Christmas. This meant I would have almost an entire year to wait and sweat over seeing them. The anticipation and fear were overwhelming. I had also ended a relationship with a girlfriend that year so my heart was truly burdened. Nonetheless I someway prepared to go home.

Around September I went to meet with my friend. I often confided in her as she knew a great deal about my past. We talked about my trip home and my concerns. And as always she listened intently and counseled me for a while. But much to my surprise, she then challenged me. She told me not to worry about going home. Her words were, "God will take care of that."

I wrote poetry and wrote for a greeting card company at the time. My friend's suggestion or challenge was for me to spend as much time in the hospitals as I could before going home. She told me to "forget about my feelings and problems and go do something for someone who is suffering." She asked me to go share my poetry, cards, and other gifts with the children and elderly on the cancer wards. I looked at her as though she were "crazy." She then responded, "I know you think this strange, but it will help. Trust me!" With a selfish attitude, I ended up taking her advice.

I spent a good amount of time visiting with patients, which proved to be very rewarding. It also took my mind off going home. I remember one night visiting with an elderly lady on the cancer ward. I sat with her and offered her one of my Christmas cards. As she read the card she smiled and thanked me. She then asked where I got the card. I told her it was mine and I wrote for the greeting card company. She smiled again and grabbed my hands.

Out of nowhere she then looked at me and said, "Son, you're hurting aren't you?" I told her no, but she then replied, "Yes, you are. I can see the pain in your eyes." I felt my eyes watering and did everything I could to stop the tears from falling. I was modestly successful. She then looked at me and said, "Don't worry about it, son. I know there are some things going on in your life and they will be OK. God is going to bless you for visiting us in the hospital." I did not think much of it, but told her thanks and went on.

When I went home for Christmas one of my abusers was the first person I saw. He immediately asked if we could talk. We did and as I discussed in my story, fortunately for me things went well.

The lesson I learned from this experience is twofold. First, regardless of our circumstances, we do not have let our own needs blind us. We sometimes have to put other people before ourselves, we have to learn to be happy for others even when we may not be, and we have to find ways to see good in our own circumstances. I spent so much time being selfish and self-centered I forgot there were other people suffering far greater pains than mine. Seeing those children and adults in the cancer ward laugh and smile was very rewarding. It was also a slap in the face. How could I complain about my life when these people were facing death every day?

Secondly, I learned that sometimes when we are in the midst of our own suffering, we still need to go about doing God's work. Not to get something in return, but simply because making that sacrifice pleases Him. When we go about doing God's work He will take care of our needs. This became so evident by the way God allowed my confrontations to go.

As always, counseling continued to be an effective strategy when dealing with my bitterness and jealousy. It helped me face my truest feelings. The more I faced my honest feelings, the easier it became along the way to give of myself, to be kind, to laugh, and to find reasons to be appreciative rather than resentful. The more of these experiences I enjoyed the more my bitterness and jealousy dissipated.

As I continued working and experiencing success with releasing my previous "guards" the impact of those successes was seen when I began facing other issues. For example, as my anger and hatred began to disappear and I began to develop my relationship with the Lord, my self-esteem and pride were both affected. I could see my self-esteem improving the most. It was so easy to see this as I began to have less of a need to impress people because I became more concerned with pleasing God. The more I felt I was able to do God's will the more satisfied I became with who I am.

Along those same lines, the more my relationship with God evolved, the more humble I became. As a result, I no longer had to be the "big man" in front of everyone and I did not have to have all of the answers. My dignity or self-respect became a positive force in my life. I learned how to believe in myself more and most importantly I learned that I was not "damaged goods." I learned to admit, yes, I was sexually abused, but that fact no longer had to define who I was.

Now, do not get me wrong, I still wanted and needed to be accepted by my family and friends. The problem was I generally sought their approval and acceptance in the wrong ways. I had to learn to be my true self by showing my true self to my intimate friends. This was of course difficult and risky because my honesty caused me to lose some friends along the way.

Learning to be and accept myself openly was a slow process. My success in this area increased as my self-esteem improved. Over time my family and friends eventually became less of a force (but no less important) in my life. This was good, because I became so dependent on them for my self-worth. As I took the pressure off them to make me feel good about myself and made it my own responsibility, I became more accepting of and enjoyed our relationships even more. Developing my relationship with God enabled me to find within my heart ample reasons to like and be myself. Psalm 146:5 states (NKJV), "Happy is he who has the God of Jacob for his help." Proverbs 16:20 also states, "Blessed is he who trusts in the LORD." I cannot over state the value of my relationship with the Lord. He was my "go to Source of strength" throughout this journey and continues to be.

As I mentioned in Chapter 6, the last issues I chose to address were my fear and learning to love. It was no coincidence I chose to tackle these issues last. It was easier to deal with the previously mentioned issues because I saw how they would help me. I did not feel threatened when addressing them. Facing my fear and learning to love on the other hand, was a completely different monster.

Fear had been such a dominant force in my life. Directly related to my abuse, I determined in my mind no one, not anyone, was going to get close enough to me in any way, to hurt me physically or emotionally again. As I discussed in my story, I learned how to be controlling and consequently sabotaged some great relationships.

Looking back I am saddened by how much my fear stopped me from getting the one thing I so desperately longed for my entire life. And that was love. I always believed I knew how to give love, but my greatest fear was receiving it. This was because if I accepted someone's love, they had power over me, which in my mind made me vulnerable. I was determined to stay as far away from anyone or anything that remotely reminded me of being vulnerable. That feeling was entirely and negatively associated with my abuse.

I remember my feelings when the relationship ended with the lady I was dating before I confronted my abusers. I was left feeling so empty because I knew to some degree it was my fault. I was trying to love her and tried to love other women with half a heart. My heart carried so much baggage there was not room for much else, especially love.

After that relationship ended I delved into a lot of self-reflection. It was very difficult admitting again how destructive my behaviors had been. I had to admit my wrongs, which meant I had to accept how much I was responsible for hurting many of the women I dated.

These facts notwithstanding, several months after my confrontations, I decided I wanted to love and receive love. This meant I had to continue on my journey to healing. But again as you can see, I did not make love a top priority, even though it was the most important thing in my heart. Looking back, I see the benefits of ridding myself from the other "guards" before trying to address my fear and learning to love. My only wish is that I had not taken so long to begin this journey.

As was the case when dealing with my bitterness, jealousy, pride, and self-esteem, I was able to see how releasing the previous guards especially anger and hatred was already impacting my fear. I mentioned my biggest fear was being vulnerable again. The reality was without my anger and hatred protecting me through violence, and my bitterness and jealousy diminishing, my heart was becoming exposed. And to that extent I was already becoming vulnerable.

In the book of 1 John 4:18 we are told, "There is no fear in love...perfect loves drives out fear." The perfect love referenced here is God's love. This scripture is a great reference point. It is a reminder that we should become so confident in God's love for us and not be afraid because He has consistently proven He will protect and provide for us.

Learning to believe in this scripture was my first strategy when dealing with my fear. It was a fairly easy strategy to adopt (even though I did not always maintain it) because as I have mentioned throughout this book, God has clearly provided for me. Most importantly, He protected me from the enemy and certainly from my own foolishness. He has shown a great love for me. Some may ask "what about the abuse?" My response to that is I have chosen to believe God has always had a plan for my life, which I believe is to participate in or provide some form of ministry in this area. I do not believe I would have the passion or compassion I have for this subject had I not experienced my own sexual abuse.

My next strategy when dealing with my fear was learning to trust. This initially became a matter of learning to trust other people, which was a big mistake. The Word of God reads in Psalm 146:3, "Do not put your trust...in mortal men." I had to learn this the hard way. By putting so much trust in people for my happiness, I gave away my own power over my circumstances. As a result, I ended up getting hurt and angry. My next option then became trusting myself, which proved to be an even bigger mistake. My tremendous fear made it unproductive for me to be left in control. This was because I would always err on the side of caution, thereby not giving myself or other people an honest chance in my relationships. The net result would typically be sabotaged and doomed relationships.

My challenge then became to find a way to have relationships with people, but not be afraid of them. Left with no viable options, my new strategy for handling my fear became putting my relationships in God's hands. I got to the point where I would and still do pray about every relationship and circumstance I am involved in. I always pray and ask God to protect me from those who wish to do me harm. I pray and ask God to protect me from myself and situations that can do me harm. In addition, I also pray and ask God for wisdom to help me see and understand His Will for my life.

Praying did not mean I would no longer get hurt in my relationships. But it did allow me to become less inclined to take things out on other people when things did not go my way. I would instead look to God for answers. I was learning to trust that His will was being done in my life, especially when things did not go my way. Psalm 9:10 tells us "those who know your name will trust in you, for you, LORD, have never forsaken those who seek you." This simply became a matter of me believing in God through my good and difficult times. And since I had many, many references in my life to choose from where God has shown He will take care of me, taking my eyes off man and trusting in God seemed to be a winning option.

Let me reiterate, releasing my "guards" was always a process. No emotion was immediately dismissed nor was I able to instantly develop a great relationship with God. All of this took time. I mentioned in the Introduction this process began in January of 1998. I am doing so much better today because I have remained true to my need for healing and true to my desire to follow God's leadership.

As time passed I began to have more positive experiences in my relationships with family and friends. This enabled me to enjoy and accept modestly loving relationships while God governed my life. But the true test of my healing, however, was going to be whether or not I would be willing to risk my heart for an intimate love.

I have learned for whatever degree of happiness we desire and regardless of our experiences, we must ultimately place a decided value on love (for self and others). This value on the emotional scale must have a monumental weight, such that our desire for happiness and our desire to give and receive love will far outweigh our consuming fear of being hurt again. For those of us who have been victims of a traumatic event, this is an agonizing decision even though we know in our hearts it is the only way we can fully enjoy a comprehensive love. We must love ourselves enough and have the courage to say yes to love and no to fear. And when we say yes to love, we must be willing to love the right way and with honesty.

Well thank God I experienced this victory. I met the most amazing young lady, who challenged and excited me like no other. As a result I was faced with my ultimate decision. Was I going to put my newly healed heart in harms way and risk being vulnerable again or was I going to run and let this great opportunity pass me by? I chose the relationship.

Before we embarked on the relationship, I shared my abuse with this young lady. My ability to share before we started dating was a clear sign a great amount of healing had taken place in my heart. I never told any woman before dating her, about my abuse. This was clearly out of fear of being rejected. Fortunately this young lady was very supportive and comforting. As a result, we continued getting to know each other and began dating very seriously.

Over time, a great love developed between us. So much so, my heart became extremely burdened with a desire to be married. The weight of this desire was the ultimate confirmation for me. When I realized I was willing to risk my newly healed heart for love and I also understood I would have to risk being made to feel vulnerable again, I knew entirely how much God had healed my heart. I was no longer afraid.

Eventually we were married. Even though the marriage unfortunately did not last, the experience did not send me spiraling backwards in an attempt to protect my heart. I still believe in love and I have a great desire to fall in love and marry again. I never thought I would be married. And certainly, I never thought I would want to try marriage a second time if the first one failed. To God be the glory.

I am not professing to be an expert on sexual abuse. I can only say that the process described in this text worked for me. It took several years and I experienced many failures along the way. I am also not saying you have to be a Christian for these concepts to work. I believe they are very practical and can be used whether you believe in God or not.

I want to say, for me, the most ironic lesson learned from my experiences is that the one thing I feared the most, being vulnerable again, actually became the one place I had to return to in order for me heal. I believe God wanted me to become vulnerable again, but to Him. Because when I got to that point, I began learning to completely depend on Him. This is where He wants us to be and this is still something I am learning to do.

Lastly, my story is about how I came to understand the very things I thought were protecting me, "my guards," were the very things ruining my life. My guards were preventing bad things or thoughts from leaving my heart and they were preventing good things and thoughts from entering my heart. With God's help I came to realize if I was going to experience any kind of happiness, "my guards" had to go.

Chapter 11

TO GOD BE THE GLORY

THIS BRINGS MY story to an end. It is my sincere hope this testimony may be the beginning of some form of healing for many victims of sexual abuse or any type of abuse. I also hope I have offered hope and inspiration with regard to the very real fact that all victims of abuse can be healed.

Before going any further I would like to note this story has been primarily about me. As I mentioned in the Introduction, the purpose of this book was not to identify or vilify my abusers. I do not see the real value in that. After all I have been through I am sure they have to be fighting with inner demons on a daily basis for the things they have done. It is kind of strange. As bad and as difficult as my life has been, I sometimes feel more sorrow and pity for the abusers than I do for myself.

Another reason I think it best not to put too much focus on the abusers is that when doing so, victims become more vulnerable. When victims focus on their abusers they can easily become consumed with being accepted or rejected by them. This in turn makes it easy for a consuming fear to develop that can prevent victims of abuse from getting on the path to healing as they are more likely to fall into traps of self-destruction by focusing more on someone or circumstances they cannot control.

I do believe abusers need to be confronted and made aware of the pain and agony they put their victims through. I also believe when possible they should be prosecuted. But ultimately, I have come to understand the bottom line is control has to be taken back from the abusers. If we are fortunate we will be granted a sincere apology that will help us on our road to healing. But again, focusing too much on the abusers would be like putting the power of my healing in someone else's hands again making it easier to get caught in webs of self-destruction.

As I mentioned in the Introduction, healing for me became a matter of first making the hard decisions as it related to me, my family, and the individuals who abused me. While making the hard decisions I had to first choose to be healed and believe that my relationship with God would enable me to endure what proved to be a long and arduous journey. But like I mentioned earlier "that which does not destroy us makes us stronger."[1]

As a result of this journey I have evolved an ever-growing personal relationship with God and I have been able to put my life in perspective. I realize that for me, in order for my life to have peace and harmony and in order for me to continue to stay on my healing path, I will have to submit my will to God's will and allow Him to captain my heart. This is not always easy to for me to do, as my will has led me to be very stubborn. But this fact notwithstanding, when I am reminded how far I have come in my life, when I look back at the many hardships and deadly traps the Lord protected me from, and when I feel the peace and joy that fills my heart each and every day, it makes it a little easier for me to try and stay humble and obedient to God's will.

I now know and can accept completely who I am. Again,

my name is Christopher Jerome Gooden and I am a recovering victim of sexual abuse. I have been molded into a man who now has self-respect; my heart and mind have been reconditioned such that I now believe in the entirety of and countless possibilities with love in my heart. I have evolved a longed for sense of self-control. I no longer see myself as damaged goods. I have forgiveness in my heart. Most importantly, I know who I am spiritually and who I am in Christ Jesus.

Before ending, I want to briefly refer back to Chapter 4. In that chapter, I mentioned how two of my closest friends, on two separate occasions, told me they were grateful for my relationship with the Lord. They were afraid "I was going to end up in prison because I had killed someone." This speaks volumes as to how much they were able to see the changes the Lord had made in my life. They knew who I was before the changes and could readily see the "new me." I have had several friends who did not know me during my struggles, to read this story. It has been amazing to hear them say "It is hard to believe you were once the person talked about in this story!" From the people who knew me throughout my journey, to those who only know the "transformed me," it is very obvious that God performed a miracle in my life. I thank Him for that and acknowledge completely the work He has done. I am a changed man living a life with joy, laughter, happiness, peace, and most importantly a satisfying love for self and others!

While I have based my story and testimony on Christian principles I hope to the extent that has been the case, you will find them to be very practical, appropriate, and believable whether you are a Christian or not. It is important when dealing with the kind of issues discussed throughout my story to have something concrete and believable to hold onto. That concrete something for me is the Word of God. For you there may be another source. Regardless of your source, healing will still require making choices, determination, and a will to fight the good fight. You must allow others to assist you along the way, maintain a measure of forgiveness, and possess an unwavering belief that your heart can change, be healed, and filled with love and happiness.

I can say this without regrets because I have been made to see where God has protected me from the enemy and from myself throughout my life. Were it not for God there is no telling where I would be this day. I perish the thought. To God alone be the glory.

NOTES

INTRODUCTION

1. Department of Health and Human Services Centers for Disease Control and Prevention Adverse Childhood Experiences (ACE) Study 2005, from Web site: www.cdc.gov/nccdphp/ace/prevalence.htm, accessed May 21, 2009.

2. Ibid.

3. From Web site: www.bartleby.com/73/1472.html, accessed May 21, 2009.

4. Friedrich Nietzsche quotation from Web site: www.brainyquote.com/quotes/authors/f/friedrich_nietzsche.html, accessed May 21, 2009.

CHAPTER 11

1. Friedrich Nietzsche quotation from Web site: www.brainyquote.com/quotes/authors/f/friedrich_nietzsche.html, accessed May 21, 2009.

But they that wait upon the Lord
shall renew their strength; they shall mount up
with wings of an eagle.

—Isaiah 40:31—

SOARING

Father God,
Be Thou
my complete strength
in the very presence
of exhausting trials and afflictions
that my wanting spirit may forever endure.

And kindly
allow a perfect peace
from a true understanding
of thy sweeping grace and mercy
like the widespread and uplifting wings
of a conquering eagle,
to unceasingly carry me
that I may through a willful obedience...
with steadfast prayer,
endless praise and joyful songs
boldly continue soaring-
high above my forthcoming storms
and faithfully remain,
amidst the sustaining winds
mercifully sent my way
from the assuring ascendancy
of thine own supreme and divine kingdom.

In the name of my Lord and Savior Jesus Christ.
Amen

CHRIS GOODEN
2001

ABOUT THE AUTHOR

A CLINICAL SOCIAL WORKER employed by the Wake County Public School System, Christopher J. Gooden attended North Carolina State University, where he earned a bachelor of arts degree in sociology with a concentration in criminal justice. His postgraduate work was completed at the University of North Carolina at Chapel Hill where he earned a masters of social work degree with a clinical concentration.

A writer of various styles of poetry, Mr. Gooden has authored a collection entitled *Look in the Mirror*, a compilation of cultural poetry addressing the social issues facing African Americans from slavery to the twentieth century. His work has been displayed at the African American Cultural Complex in Raleigh, North Carolina and The Haiti Heritage Center in Durham, North Carolina. Mr. Gooden is the author of a self-published book of romantic poetry entitled Loves' Shadows and also writes for a local greeting card company.

Mr. Gooden lives in Raleigh, North Carolina. He attends Watts Chapel Missionary Baptist Church. A member of Kappa Alpha Psi fraternity, he enjoys golf, bowling, movies, and writing.

TO CONTACT THE AUTHOR

christophergooden@gmail.com